CW01464076

THE POETRY GAMES: TRUTH OR DARE?

VOICES FROM THE MIDLANDS

Edited By Daisy Job

First published in Great Britain in 2018 by:

YoungWriters
Est. 1991

Young Writers
Remus House
Coltsfoot Drive
Peterborough
PE2 9BF
Telephone: 01733 890066
Website: www.youngwriters.co.uk

All Rights Reserved
Book Design by Ben Reeves
© Copyright Contributors 2017
SB ISBN 978-1-78896-122-6
Printed and bound in the UK by BookPrintingUK
Website: www.bookprintinguk.com
YB0348H

FOREWORD

Welcome to *The Poetry Games: Truth Or Dare? - Voices From The Midlands*.

For this poetry competition we encouraged self-expression from secondary school pupils through a truth or dare format. The 'truth' entries reveal what the writer is passionate about, offer a sincere expression of their emotions or share their hopes, dreams and ambitions. The 'dare' entries are provocative in order to question the conventional and voice the writer's opinion; they may fight for their beliefs in verse or just tell a poetic tale of an audacious adventure.

We encouraged the writers to think about the technical aspects of their poems' compositions, whether they be an acrostic, haiku, free verse or another form, and to consider techniques such as metaphors, onomatopoeia, rhyme and imagery.

I'm so impressed with both the content and the style of the poems we received and I hope you enjoy them as much as I have. I'd like to congratulate all the writers who entered this competition and took up the challenge to join Team Truth or Team Dare.

Enjoy!

CONTENTS

Amber Wilson (11)	71
Emily Harris (14) & Ottie	72
Barney Brass (13)	73
Henry Price (11)	74
Christopher Austin	76
Christopher Arthur (11)	77
Harvey Bridgeman	78
Ryan Benjamin Frost (11)	79
Lucas Willson (11)	80
Nico Anderson (15)	81
Daniel Bennett (11)	82
Chloe Deakin (11)	83
Bethany Clinton	84
Max Elkin	85
Reece Sutherland (11)	86
Adam (13) & Christian	87
Robinson (13)	
Jessica Martin	88
Morgan Steventon (11)	89
Jacob Murray (15)	90
Hayden Burrows (14)	91
Elijah Hayes (11)	92

Lincoln University Technical College, Lincoln

Aron John Brydon (14)	93
Ethan Ward	94
Jack Armitage (14)	97
Regan King (14)	98
Nicole Scrupps (14)	100
Jack Hatcher (14)	103
Leon Jake Goodhew (14)	104
Alexandra Senkiw-Smith (14)	106
Kati Louise Robinson (15)	108
Ben Rodgers (14)	111
Paris Jessie Layzell (14)	112
Shaun Cozens (14)	114
Grace Harley (14)	116
Mark Bradshaw (14)	118
Rachel Odlin (14)	120
Ben Edward Davis (15)	122
Callum Benfield (14)	124
Georgia Stevenson (14)	126

Edward Ruddock (14)	128
Spencer Beeson (14)	130
Ethan Richardson (14)	132
Luke Foster (14)	133
Mitchell Mays (14)	134
Siobhan Watson (15)	135
Ryan Arnold (15)	136
Kyle Fox (14)	137
Eloise Winterflood (14)	138
Ayrton Alan Rowley (14)	139
Jordi Folland (15)	140
Liam Parks (15)	141
Clio Mackay (14)	142
Alex Castleman (15)	143
Paulius Rimkus (14)	144
Leo Johns-Wait (14)	145
Leo Alexander Hodson (15)	146
Joseph Ager (14)	147
Saffron Hartley (15)	148
Brett Jordan MacDonald (14)	149
Isabelle Hughes (14)	150
Austin Alexander Bridgman (15)	151
Cameron Young (14)	152
Courtney Killingsworth (15)	153

Manor House School, Ashby-De-La-Zouch

Myla Parsons-Smith (12)	154

Mount St Mary's College, Spinkhill

Lucy Cockell (11)	155
Elliot Parker (11)	156
Jenson Cole (11)	158
Sam Stacey (11)	159
Alex Jakeman (11)	160
Evie C Bounds (11)	161
Luigi Lancaster-Simper (11)	162
Matthew Fidler (11)	163
Christopher Penny (11)	164
Abraham Murra (12)	165
Henry Renshaw (11)	166

THE POEMS

WEATHER CHANGES

Truth

W inter is the time I can barely feel my roots,

 E specially because it's so cold,

 A cloud is soaring through the sky in peace,

 T he sun, a blazing hot fiery sphere keeping the Earth warm,

 H eat steaming on our wooden branches,

 E nding years are about to come,

 R ainbows end near me and that is where treasure's found.

 C loudy days always give me a slight shiver down my spine,

 H ailstones are sometimes shot down from the sky

 A utumn always steals my leaves making me leafless,

 N ight is so dark that there is no light to keep me safe,

 G narled roots are making it hard for me to absorb water,

 E legant stars are always so bright which brings me light,

 S hade always seems to cover me from the weather.

Claudia Anton (13)

TRUTH

THE GAMES GUARDIAN

Dare

Drip, drip, below the bridge,
Where a man sleeps on the ridge.
By the grass is where he lay,
Waiting on that summer day.
Yet his face was not man at all,
It was crumpled, ugly, scary, small.
Tangled hair licked his head,
Like seaweed from the riverbed.

A passing maiden heard the drip,
Climbing down the bank - 'don't slip'.
She heard the voice and turned aside,
Blushing like a wedding bride.
A handsome man with glossy hair,
Stood there in his underwear!
She took his hand and walked uphill,
standing at the top, stone still.

'I must go,' the maiden said,
And swiftly turned away her head.
'Wait' the man pleaded, half nude,
'Stay for a game, don't be rude'.

DARE

The maiden thought for a while,
And finally agreed with a curious smile.
What game is it? she thought,
Mother is about, I can't be caught.

He read her mind just at that time,
And spoke his next words all in rhyme:
'Truth or dare is what we'll play,
Pick one and I'll be on my way.
Don't try to run for I am quicker,'
Just then his hair did try to lick her.
His face grew smaller and uglier still,
Until a troll stood on that hill.

'Truth or Dare what will you pick?'
'I can't believe this wicked trick!'
The maiden tried to call for help,
But found her voice was just a yelp.
'Fine! Fine! I'll play your game,
But you must play a round the same!'
The troll then stood and scratched his head,
And agreed to the deal with a sense of dread.

'I pick Truth,' the maiden spoke,
The troll just then began to choke.
'Um... um... just let me think!'
The maiden smiled and gave a wink.
'No, you will do a dare for me,
I'm your ruler, bend the knee!'

DARE

The troll at once began to shiver,
below his waist his legs did quiver.

'I know you must do what I ask,
You set the rules and that's your task!'
The troll then fell upon the floor,
His body shaking more and more.
His troll complexion began to crack,
and suddenly the man was back.
So they moved into a village nearby there,
And promised each other to never again, play Truth or Dare!

Benjamin Jacob Garwood (17)

DARE

UNTITLED

Truth

The day I visited the zoo when I was little
I was excited to see the zoo
I never expected to see them all locked up in tiny cages
Whilst we pulled faces at them
The day I went to the zoo
I never imagined that animals were used for
our entertainment
And I never realised how depressed they were when they
were clearly taken from their family
The day I went to the zoo I never knew that animals would
spend the rest of their lives in captivity
When all they dream of is roaming free
The day I went to the zoo I wanted to set all the animals
free
And I wanted them to be happy
The day I went to the zoo
I decided that no animal should be treated this way
When I went to the zoo
I knew what animals deserved to be free.

Amy Torr (17)

TWO OF A KIND

Dare

Who has seen Truth? Not me,
That who lives on Dare alone,
Ambition and chance and luck all too less
For a life thrillingly, spiritedly alive,
Full of risk, yes, but adventure
Oh! Could you resist (if you'd excuse the pun)
The truest temptation;
To leave this world behind
Start anew, once more a child
But this time you'll be a daring one:
Unbounded by what is deemed right
Unhindered by what one might say is wrong,
Like me,
The one who dares to live,
And yet, for all this I don't know what Truth is.

Shall I chance a Dare? Not I,
One who lives in the reign of Truth
Verity, sincerity, God - call it what you may,
A humble life that is little understood
Full of wisdom, and fully content...
Consider this (and I'll ask you only this once)
You must dare yourself;
To leave this world behind
Start anew, once more a child

DARE

But this time you'll be a truthful one:
Motivated by righteousness and justice
Ever journeying with compassion and love,
Like I do,
The one who's true at heart,
And yet, perhaps a dare is a good way to start.

Shubhangi Bhatt (16)

THE LIFE OF A CROCODILE

Dare

I am a young crocodile
I still have a bright future
I still have a chance of leading a better life
I can dive, I can swim and I can still do anything
But the poachers are ready to ruin everything
They come roaming into my territory and they try to kill me
They try to shoot me so that they can make all sorts of things out of me
Like bags and shoes... all out of my skin
Then my life turned into a tiring, horrid one
All because of the hunters

I am an old crocodile
I had a fun and beneficial life in the past
I now just want to have a relaxing life
I just want to rest
But the hunters are searching for me
They want to kill me and use me up for their bags and other stuff
And I can't move quickly, so they find me
Finally, I'm a dead animal, skin used for those humans' things

DARE

Why? Why do you come attacking me and my family?
Of what benefit are bags from my skin to you?
Why do you want to ruin my life?
Would you like it if you were attacked and killed?
Stop coming! Stop stealing my life and my future!
I am here to live... just like *you*!

Hafsah Saleem (11)

TAKE A WALK WITH ME?

Truth

Take a walk with me,
To a place where we can be safe together?
Take a walk with me,
To a place where we can be free forever?
To a place where numbers are numbers
A place where names are names
Where love conquers all
And fear is nothing to fear at all

Take a walk with me
Deep into the wood?
Where you and I can just be
Together, every day like we should
Take a walk with me
Hand in hand
Across the stream
Down through our land

Won't you come with me
To a place where our love can be eternal?
Won't you come with me
To a place where we can scream and shout?
To a place where I can kiss you

TRUTH

But I'll never have to miss you
Like Cathy and Heathcliff, upon the moors
Forever and always, I am yours

So take a walk with me
To a place far away
Take a walk with me
Where I am yours at night and day
Take a walk with me
To a place where we can be safe together
Take a walk with me
To a place where we are free forever.

Millie Beck (17)

A HELPING HAND

Truth

The eyes through which others see,
Will always be a mystery,
No one knows or dares to ask,
What's hidden beneath that happy mask,
People hide and people feel shame,
They feel like they're the ones to blame,
For everything and all the pain,
Now stop, just think, by feeling like this, what are you going to gain?

Something has to change, but what?
Ideas link together like a dot to dot,
Thoughts run round like in the Wild West,
Until you realise you've finished your quest,
Take my advice and read it slow,
Why don't you possibly give it a go?

Look at the stars they're shining bright,
Just like your future beyond this beautiful night,
Don't take any notice of what people say,
Just let all the negative thoughts drift away,
When life gets tough and you're feeling low,
Just picture happy things and let them show,
Building confidence is one of the number one things,
Just sit tight and spread your wings,

TRUTH

You'll always have a helping hand,
Just find the courage, get up, and stand.

Charlotte Warren (17)

IS A GUN YOUR ONLY STRENGTH?

Dare

When you wake up do you think of a gun?
Do you have a gold or bronze conscience?
Your legs are moving but your heart is asleep.
Your mouth is your resilience.
Your hand is your armour.
You're a lion with worries.
But you're a beast for desire.

Your head is consumed with blood.
But your hand is a virgin.
You repent when they're light.
You fall back to actions when it's dark.
Your victims look at you with disgust.
Their lips begging for mercy.

(One girl and one guy) with hopes and dreams.
Pleading to a belief they despised.
Squeezing your victim's hand so tightly it's red.
Closing your bruised eyes to see a glimpse of sunlight.
All you see is your blood splattered on the face of your killer.

Your prey will never know happiness.
Their decayed bodies will be left on the devil's floor.
While you will slowly kill yourself with a cigar.

DARE

Why don't you do the right thing instead?
Live the right life.
Rather than pulling the trigger.

Angel Kpodoh (13)

AN AUTUMN LEAF

Truth

Towering trees,
Golden, burnt orange leaves,
Twirl and dance in the autumn breeze,
Jealous of the coming girl,
The way she ambles through the woodland,
Head tilted high,
Confidence in her every step,
Leaving a luminous trail in her wake,
Her eyes; sparkling stars,
The shade of acorns and warm sienna,
Hiding her agony away,
They don't see her soul is shattering,
Like jagged slivers of ice,
They don't see the bravery washing away
In those gem-like tears,
They don't see her trying to hide,
Behind a mask of coping,
And then she stops,
Catching the sight of a leaf,
Somehow different to the others,
Beautiful, bronze, brittle,
Pirouetting its way down,
An invisible swirl of gust,
She smiles,

TRUTH

Lighting up the forest, like wildfire,
She clutches the leaf,
Whispering her secret,
Finally letting go...

Rabeea Bhatti (13)

MIND

Truth

They're always watching you, them up there
With their steady walk and their silky hair
Shapeless and transient, they wander around
Sometimes unseen, rarely touching the ground

Never really noticed, as they spin and they play
Not heading anywhere, but sometimes they stay
The more you ignore them, the more they appear
Angry and sad, they shed silent tears

We fall asleep, there aren't many to see
They sometimes darken, begin to disagree
You know it's the one, your dreams do not lie
A bolt of white lightning across a black night sky

They rumble and fight as they float, taking flight
And the world goes dark and they block out the light
Swirling and twirling, a hurricane of unkind
Stopped by the truth of this expanse, called the mind

Jamie Kirkland (14)

TRUTH

TRUTH OR DARE?

Dare

The meaning of the word 'truth' had always meant a lot,
My mother used to say it every night before I rested my head,
Trust, believe the truth.

And I had always believed it,
I never told a lie,
I was a goody two shoes.
At least I was.
Until someone told me otherwise.
Until someone told me about dare.

We moved house,
I had new friends who were more exciting, adventurous.
I thought they were amazing, I had never been on an adventure.

My first one was on Halloween,
But I can only say one thing,
I told a lie,
A very big lie,
A lie that changed my future.
It began with a dare.
Which would you pick?
Truth or dare?

Izabella Roberts (12)

DARE

YoungWriters

TESTING ON ANIMALS IS WRONG

Truth

I think testing on animals is wrong.
Animals have no voice on the matter,
They are trapped by us and carried along.
To do this to them we are mad hatters.
Even if things tried on them are safe for them,
How do we know that they are safe for us?
This cruelty I just have to condemn!
This is something that we should all discuss.
Why is it we feel the need to do this,
To send poor animals to their sad fate?
Yet the animals' pain we all dismiss,
When the advantages are not that great.
Why do we do this to such a small voice?
Why can't we stop this and make the right choice?

Sarah Murphy

TRUTH

SAVE OUR PLANET

Truth

Things have gone wrong
Everyone should stop thinking that
Nurturing our Earth is going to restore it
A sense deep down tells me
Lust doesn't have the capacity to restore our home
People are constantly repeating that

Replanting trees is pathetic
Unbelievably, our society believes that
Our environment can still be saved

Eventually, the human race may realise that
Venturers are decreasing and our generation is less
infatuated
After all, we are going to lose our home because
Simple-minded actions done by us have ruined a prodigious
paradise

(Now read it from bottom to top).

Elizabeth Martini (14)

TRUTH

OPINIONATED WAR

Truth

I've seen the battles,
That separated us;
I've seen the error of the ways.

It's.
Not.
Right.
I've watched
And mourned
And cried with grief,
And now,
Now, I realise.

Conscientious pacifism it may seem,
But I don't
Care.

Think, how many died?

Did you see their faces,
Hear their last sodden words?
'Mother...'

No, I didn't think so.
You sit and watch and
Shout and laugh.
Talk, talk, talk.

TRUTH

You don't know how it feels.
War is wrong.
No matter what you think.

It's not right,
And we all know it, deep down.

Beth Llewellin (13)

THE CHICKEN NUGGET OF DOOM

Dare

There once was a nugget of doom
Who wanted to take over the world
He climbed up a broom and into a smelly room
There was a bee flying happily and free
The nugget of doom shot it down with ketchup
Then stole its wings and escaped KFC
He made an army of chickens and fries
That lasts until he dies and his army cries
They shot each other, even if you were their brother
Ketchup everywhere, even in your underwear
A burger nuke ended the war
But the dead fries and chicken on the floor
Were swept away by a soda tsunami.

Lewis Morgan-Barrett

DARE

DISTANT, YET SO FOND

Truth

Distant. Yet somehow so fond,
I remember the lively atmosphere,
The laughs, the smiles and the jokes that occurred,
A room which was once filled with happiness and
tranquillity,
The freedom which we had,
The atmosphere: so sweet and serene,
The light shining upon our faces,
We were content, laughing and happy,
With smiles on our faces,
The sound of our laughter filling the room,
Mistakes forgotten,
Arguments aside,
Worries washed away,
The hours ticking by,
The days flicking by,
The months dripping by,
Now it all seems like a blur.

Alishba Begum (17)

TRUTH

ART

Truth

Pencil to paper,
Marks from the eraser.
Paint on brush,
Spilt in a rush.
Open the book,
It's creased, look!
Ink for the fountain pen,
Splodges on the table then.
Colouring still to do,
White gaps left by who?
Coincidences you start to see,
Was it you or was it me?
Mistakes is what we talk about,
Sometimes because of doubt.
You can't do much at the end of the day,
So carry on in the same way.
It is just the start,
For this is art...

Sofia Ambrosi (12)

TRUTH

HOPE

Truth

What's always there but no one can see?
The thing that makes us, you and me
It can be held onto
With dreams in hand
But never touched
Or it will topple like sand
It grants us wishes
Magical and true
It comes when you need it
A virtue to you
And if you lose it
Nothing will matter
It should come back strong
Bigger and better
It conquers the fears
Of this elegant world
And when your life ends
It will be free as a bird...

Vil Borodi (12)

NOTICE ME?

Dare

Deserted in the abyss of water, it lay
Glinting, yet melting in the scorching light of the sun

Twisting and turning,
Unable to get anywhere

Trapped in rings of plastic,
Sharp enough to create a river of blood

Enveloped by anguish,
Its heart growing denser by the second

Slowly dying, losing hope,
Waiting and waiting to be noticed

Nobody sees it falling to sleep,
And never awakening.

Jyotsna Jayanth Bhat (14)

DARE

PARALYSIS OF THE HUMAN MIND

Dare

A fiery cascade will form from my head to my fists
Thoughts.
Actions.
Scattered.
Red-hot burns my throat
So, scorched become my mouth,
A hotbed for paralysis
My words take flight but are shot
By my oppressor's arrow.
Anger explodes inside my chest
I begrudgingly drag my carcass.

Clare Serugo (16)

MYSTERY PERSONA

Truth

Who am I?
My eyelids flutter and take me
Away to a crystallised, azure sky
To my left, a grand oak tree
Its great branches spindly and gnarled
Trying to reach the silken fabric of the sky
To my right, a vast, empty meadow
Glimmering with sunshine that trickles
Down on the petals of delicate, dancing flowers
I can feel the soft grass beneath my body
It makes me feel so adrenalised
Yet I cannot move my body at all
For as long as I can remember
I have never exhibited human emotions
Perhaps it is because I am an alien foreigner
To this land and to people's hearts
Memories, peculiar things that are spun
Into careful webs of your brain
It's a shame that the spider in my mind
Weaves and then shatters
The fragile illusion of my remaining memories

TRUTH

One more, blink
I am on a cold, snowy mountain
The dagger-like, icy wind spears through my plain clothes
I have noticed that I'm in uniform
That is quite an interesting thing
I believe that, while wearing this
I have begun to make a distant, cloudy memory
Of a friendship - I believe that that was the word
A bond that is unseeable to the eye, but
Viewable to the heart
Useless to spite
But useful for love
With another blink
I am in... where am I?
Are these my fears?
Unrecognisable in a dense, dark forest of
Black and silence
So eerie that I felt that I was disappearing
Out of sight, out of memories, out of life
Snap out of it! Pull yourself together
I cannot let this emotion overwhelm me!
All I have to do is
Blink
I am in a more comfortable place now
A warm red glow envelops me and I see
The broken pieces of web, scattered across the seamless
existence

TRUTH

A spectrum is formed and the memories stick to me
Like a dewdrop to a spider's web

My black widow is grieved and dying
However
Her child lives on in me
Its first web will take some years but
It will be fine
As I watch as the glow is torn open
By the spider's hooked, shivering leg
I know one thing
I am unique
I am devoted to this new life
Although that thing that I had done
Cannot be undone
I will redeem myself
But my last thought before I enter my life is that
Only I will know what happened before
And that torture will never cease
No matter what happens
No matter what my efforts are to destroy my life
The black widow's web will always be there
No matter what I do
I will remember the haunting curse
Of my previous life
And all of its worst fears.

Kareish Rajkanna
Bourne Grammar School, Bourne

TRUTH

SO HIGH

Truth

I was so high in the baby-blue sky
In my air balloon that was exploding with colours
Birds kissing me on my dimples
The wind hugging my little soul

I was so high in the baby-blue sky
As I saw below me
The fresh green moss that was dancing for the sun's
spotlight
Blooming buds embellished the paradise my little eyes saw
As the glittering beads of light awakened all its children
from Mother Nature's soul

I was so high in the baby-blue sky
When I saw the blue honey of the Mediterranean
Diamonds had been studded into the blue
To cleanse and wash the golden blanket
The mother of the ocean was teaching its droplets to dance
in glee and pride
The ripples of blue sing a melody for the mother of the
ocean
Such a beauty, such a beauty
I felt so high in the baby-blue sky...

Sandra Sajosh (14)
Bourne Grammar School, Bourne

TRUTH

DEMONS

Dare

(Written to highlight the gap in mental health support for adolescents. If you feel this way, please seek help from a professional.)

Battles aren't always shown
They may be silent
They may be battles with ourselves
Or battles with our demons

My demons grew as they pushed me lower
They pushed me into their comforting arms
Their spindly arms
They comforted me

The demons controlled my thoughts
The demons controlled my movements
The demons controlled each escaped tear
The demons controlled me

I was trapped
I realised too late
They had pushed me into a trap
The demons comforted me

They followed every tear
They made more flow

DARE

They didn't know my own battle
The battle that was silent

No one knew my battle
Maybe they should
Would they judge me?
Would they believe me?

Why can't we talk about this?
Why is talking about silent battles wrong?
Would they judge me?
Would they believe me?

What if I did talk?
Would my demons shrink?
Or would they grow?
I'm running out of time

Should I talk?
Should I stay silent?
There's no more time
My demons are too strong

The only way to live is to kill my demons
The only way to kill them is to end myself
So, I killed them.

Gabbie Jade Fleury (15)
Charles Read Academy, Corby Glen

I LIVED IN AFGHANISTAN

Truth

Hello my name is Wasil Fatehkhail.
I was born in Afghanistan.
My house was very big.
There were trees of apple, cherries, plums and more.
My school was bad in Afghanistan because
the teachers were beating the children with a stick.

My favourite place was my garden
because there were fruits everywhere in the garden.
I love the month July because it is the hottest month of the year.
One thing I don't like about Afghanistan is that there
is fighting in every city.
I like Afghanistan because my grandparents are living there
and I was born there.

I came to England in December 2012.
I travelled by plane with my family.
One good thing about moving to England was I could go to school.

However
The sad thing about moving to England was that I missed
my country and my friends.

TRUTH

I don't like the weather in Birmingham.
I like Birmingham because the buses are very good.
Birmingham has good places to do shopping and places for
fun.

I like my school in Birmingham because the teachers do not
beat us like in Afghanistan.
In my school the students are too noisy.

My favourite subjects are
English, maths, geography and science

I will do ESOL for the first year in the college.
My future is to be a pilot.

Wasil Fatehkail (15)

Cockshut Hill Technology College, Yardley

ORDINARY LIFE

Truth

Ordinary life is my condemnation
I just want to tragically
Observe the prettiest things
From the stars' point of view

I want to blindly fall
Into gorgeous chaos and
Seductively destroy my perfect character
Creating a masterpiece

Ordinary life is my damnation
I just want to unexpectedly
Rain down violently
On all creation

I want to hide
The beautiful sunrise and
Create an extraordinary
Never-ending night

I want to be a striking sinner
Bur secretly play the pure saint
Yet, I don't want any of this
Truthfully, I just want to sleep
And dream all this again.

Alexandra Lacatusu (14)
Cockshut Hill Technology College, Yardley

TRUTH

WAR

Dare

It was a noble cause they say
The death, the pain, pure loss
They say they died for a reason
That reason's left unsaid

For we lined up our young men
Then shot them through the head
We killed them for a simple feud
The world can never forget

Those that didn't die
They're still where chaos reigns
They say they're finding peace
For those millions, it's still hell

It was a righteous cause they say
The death, the pain, the rage
But war brings loss to thousands
Peace destroyed for greed

Syria's all but gone
A pitted shell, no more
War's reduced to rubble
Considerable beauty of before

Now all that lives is cruelty
Guns, bombs and more

Refugees flood out, escape!
But there's no escaping war.

Joseph David Isaac Ducille (12)
Elmhurst School For Dance In Association With Birmingham Royal Ballet,
Birmingham

DARE

OPINIONS MATTER

Dare

I gathered all the geeks, freaks, my peeps around
Said, 'The bullies always take our ground,
that pound, don't let them bring you down!'
'We need to rebel, they dominate the school!'
One shouted, 'No more labels, the school's unstable, it's not cool!'
And so we did, the next day - no one will ever take our privileges away!
Nope, not today, no leading astray, we shout, 'Hooray,' we slay, time to obey!
The bullies ran away screamin',
'They're the cowards, the school's outs,
no more bullies being sour, the downers, we won!'
The deed's done, it was fun, now nobody's shunned,
the bullies were hit hard as a ton!
Teachers are powerless, get devoured!

Cosma Jade Fansa (11)
Kesteven & Grantham Girls' School, Grantham

DARE

DOESN'T HAVE TO END THIS WAY

Truth

Under the light of a cold, heartless moon,
Two lovers meet to consummate their unspoken vows.
The first, the Eccedentesiast, a master of illusion
Who hides their pain behind a painted smile,
Smiles genuinely - one that makes their eyes twinkle.

The second is plagued with seed of dread
That eats at their heart and messes with their head.
Thanatophobia - the fear of losing someone you love.
But their storms of worry are calmed with the sight
Of their dearest companion safe at their side.

A soft lullaby of the summer wind
Rustles through woven strands of dead grass;
The lovers lay flush against one another
And the air around them is alive.
The weight of the world presses down around them
As the humid day changes to a stifling night.

Somewhere in the distance, a metal man -
Smelted from the fires of tradition,
Crafted by the hands of ignorance and denial -
Talks to a crowd of equal-minded machines,

TRUTH

Condemning the lovers, condemning their lives,
Condemning their beliefs and their very existence.

But they don't care.
They don't care for the summer heat,
They don't care for the summer hate.
They have no time for cruel words,
Syllables sharpened with deadly precision,
Consonants carved with knives of irrational anger -
All intended to stab and cut and slice
And hurt and maim and kill -
They do not care.

Even as the words of the metal man
Poisons the water the wooden men drink from,
Killing off their roots - corrupting them,
Turning them against one another;
The lovers do not care.
They know they have each other.

Even as the grass they lay in pricks at their skin,
And is crunched beneath the boots of more metal men,
Come to corrupt, come to kill,
The lovers do not care.
They knew it would end this way.

But... it didn't have to end this way -
Doesn't have to end this way.

The light of a full moon -
Full like the hearts of the people below it -
Shines upon two lovers, meeting in a lush field,
To consummate their vows they proclaimed to a crowd,
In a world where there are no metal men
With machines of terror,
With words designed to destroy.

But now the lovers sleep in a blissful eternity,
Their ears deaf to the words of abuse around them,
Their eyes blind to the scorn and disgust.
They only have eyes for each other, as they rest
Safe in each other's arms.

It didn't have to end this way.
And that's the truth.

Alexandra Tyndall (16)
Kesteven & Grantham Girls' School, Grantham

TRUTH

YOU CANNOT CHANGE IT

Dare

You cannot change it
It has been done
The fighting is over
But the battle is still not won
Will it come into next generations?
Fighting, squabbling, killing and all
What will be next?
Maybe the building of a big wall
Lots of blood spilt
Fine young men killed
All over power
Oh, we're so thrilled
People were poisoned
People were shot
People would die
Their memories would rot
Who are we to do such a thing
Our world was so good
Before we destroyed it
Doing all we could
Families cried
Leaders laughed

DARE

Soldiers hurt
How could we have been so daft?
So just think
Before you declare
That all will be a war
Think, is it really fair?
Or should you just leave us alone
To get on with our lives
So that we can't moan?

Skye Searle (11)
Kesteven & Grantham Girls' School, Grantham

DARE

FOR ETERNITY

Truth

In the reflection of my journeys,
I find myself missing from the memories
Of people I don't see.
I myself am missing from places I've never been
Or ever will be
Because you won't be there with me.
Why do you cage me
In these walls, alone with the poison of my mind
That I drink to delude me
Into insanity?
So that I may pretend to float in the illusion of false ecstasy,
Where you will never be?
Your voice sounded like beautiful melodies
That echoed in the forest among the waterfalls and trees.
Hypnotising me by being so harmonic and sweet.
And when moonlight lent itself as music
We saw the starlight with clarity.
I felt tethered to existence by you like gravity.
Love bloomed.
It felt other worldly.
Or so I thought before I became disillusioned by reality.
For you did not feel the same as me,
Despite my affection being verity.
You placed my love on the wrong side of morality

But still if you asked, 'How I love thee?'
I would say, 'For eternity.'

Amna Naeem (17)
Kesteven & Grantham Girls' School, Grantham

TRUTH

SPEAK UP!

Dare

Why is it that this world just can't get along
Somewhere in the world we just have to have grudges
Why can't we all just live in safety and reassurance?
Not fear where we all hide out of sight
Speak up is what we need to do
Speak up is what we need to live up to!

Why must others not be allowed to sing their song
Somehow I know we won't let it swallow our pride
Why is it we all choose to run and hide?
I know that half of this world has opinions, beliefs
That all have a chance to be heard
Maybe not all will see, but believe me
Speak up, for maybe just you, she and he
Speak up and someone might just see

Why is it that I have to follow rules?
Somebody is dying to break free
Why should I be like all the rest?
I want to be free, make my own rules
Not follow everyone else
Stop being so blind! Live your life
Speak up and you never know
Speak up and let it show!

DARE

Now I have chosen to be me
Let others know and truly see
If some just can't seem to get it into their heads
Don't waste your time slipping through the threats!
Truly be the best and reach your full potential
Speak up as it is extremely essential!
Speak up, you will be heard!

Madeline Sharman (13)

Kesteven & Grantham Girls' School, Grantham

DARE

KNOW YOUR PLACE

Dare

Boys, throw on your jersey
Girls, put on your dress
Girls, keep it all tidy
Boys, make it a mess

Girls, slap on the make-up
Boys, slip on the tie
Boys, make it all up
Girls, don't say a lie

Do all these things and no one gets hurt

Boys, ask out the girls
Girls, be flattered by his words
Girls, be the geeks
Boys, be the nerds

Girls, have a squabble
Boys, have a fight
Boys, buy just this and that
Girls, buy everything in sight

Do all these things and no one will fight

What if these changed?
Each side acted as one?

DARE

No, all hell would unleash
Like a war never to be won

Boys, put on your dress
Girls, throw on your jersey
Girls, make a mess
Boys, make it all tidy

Girls, slip on the tie
Boys, slap on the make-up
Boys, don't say a lie
Girls, make it all up

Do all these things and everyone gets hurt

Boys, be flattered by her words
Girls, ask out the boys
Girls, be the nerds
Boys, be the geeks

Girls, have a fight
Boys, have a squabble
Boys, buy everything in sight
Girls, buy just this and that

Do all these things and everyone will fight
Doesn't sound right
Like a blow
Or bite
To everything we know.

Evie Romana Milford (14)

Kesteven & Grantham Girls' School, Grantham

DARE

BEAST ATTACK

Truth

He's always there lurking in the darkness
Hiding in the crowds, hiding in the problems
There with me when I have to do presentations
There when I have to talk to new people

Suddenly he grabs me, tighter, closer
Can't breathe, can't speak
Why do you do this every time? I think
Hyperventilating, can't breathe, can't breathe
He pulls me further down the hole
I think of past mistakes, everything's gone wrong with my life
Too scared... shaking
Alone, so alone
Too scared, can't breathe

He releases his grip, I can breathe
Catching my breath
Deep breaths in and out
Calming down
My own demon steps away

He whispers his name...
'Anxiety.'
And steps back next to me and
I wonder when he will next taunt me.

Freya Owen (15)
King Edward VI High School, Stafford

TRUTH

HOMEWORK

Dare

I like school, don't get me wrong, I do,
But homework, oh homework
I hate it, I do.

The thought of homework makes me drool,
I sit down thinking that this is not like primary school.
Who even invented this tedious chore?
Whoever it was, needs to be told that it is such a bore.

I like school, don't get me wrong, I do
But homework, oh homework
I hate it, I do.

Lost in a dream I stare out the window,
Not knowing if my words will flow.
The rolling hills and fields stare right at me,
I should be out there playing, I know.
No longer can I enjoy the long warm day,
So now I am left feeling grey.

I like school, don't get me wrong, I do
But homework, oh homework
I hate it, I do.

As the deadline starts to loom,
Fear and panic takes hold of the room.
Content? Presentation? Is there enough?

DARE

The answer to which, is always tough.
I soldier on, sensing the end
Finishing touches, it's finished, ready to send.

I like school, don't get me wrong, I do
But homework, oh homework
I hate it, I do.

It's gone, finally gone,
But now another one takes its place.
Will this chore help me do well?
Only time will tell!

Ben Dean (11)
King Edward VI High School, Stafford

MY FOREVER PUP

Truth

At ten years old, I came home to
Find you in my living room,
Full of love since day one;
Our lives together have just begun.
We've known each other for half a year
And in that time I've shed some tears.
But you've been there, every time
Cheering me up, and bringing sunshine.
You don't know how much you're loved
My loyal, funny, forever pup.
When we're together, I hope you know
How much I care and love you so.
When you get sick I'll comfort you
Just like you do when I am blue.
Don't be afraid of the vet my pup
They're helping you to get back up,
So we can have some fun once more
Shouting at the postman at the door,
Chasing tails and fetching balls,
Getting Mum mad when we run in the halls.
And when you're too old to play anymore
And you sit at my feet on the floor,
I'll whisper in your ear and stroke your head
As we remember the times that we had:

TRUTH

Running in the park, chasing cats
Digging up dirt, barking at the bat.
And when all that's left is your empty bed
I'll replay those memories in my head
And the love you gave till we had to part
I'll keep forever in my heart.

Paris Gore (11)
King Edward VI High School, Stafford

I LOVED YOU

Truth

You have been the best friend anyone could ask for,
I loved you and you loved me.
We did everything together,
we laughed, we fought and we fell closer together by the
minute,
I loved you.

As we grew older, we grew further apart
We didn't talk, we didn't walk, and we didn't perceive our
future.
Away you went, further away from my touch
I missed you,
I loved you.

Adults we became, moving on with our lives
Talking became a regular thing between us although our
past was left behind,
The truth is you were loved, you stole my heart, I stole your
childhood,
I loved you.

Even older we grew, our hairs turning grey,
Families stood by us, happy with their lives
I remember your touch lay upon my cheek, making my heart
warm, even though my body was like ice.
Even older we became, and our age became a problem,

TRUTH

Coughing, headaches, and all the illnesses you had
But nothing could bring you down
Until
Slowly, slowly, we drifted away. Together
Goodbye
I loved you.

Zara Bell (11)
King Edward VI High School, Stafford

MY PETS

Truth

Introduction to my pets
Yes, they have visited the vets

Mac spends all his day on his back
He likes playing with socks but he can't pick locks

Lola, who doesn't like Coca-Cola
Bites your bum if you don't fill her tum

Paw's claws don't follow any laws
She is very vocal and annoys all the locals

Charlie's a cheeky chappy
Even though he doesn't look very happy

Revels, like the sweet treats
Always takes my seat

Twix who licks is a naughty tortie
Like her sister she ain't got no mister

Flynn and Fitz, are our new recruits
And they are wearing ginger suits

Last but no means least, is Rosie Posie
A Labrador who's very nosy

This is my collection of pets
Please don't judge because they are the best

TRUTH

I bet you now want a pet
And I think you should, the deal is set.

Jorja Alex Lea (12)
King Edward VI High School, Stafford

SCHOOL MAYHEM

Truth

The rolling pencils, the clicking pens
The silence screams till the lesson ends
Chairs sliding on the floor
People rushing through the door
Mumbles echo in the halls
People's names being called
Weave through the tight crowd
Brace yourself, it's getting loud
A mumble turns into a shout
Quick you need to get out
You take a left, you take a right
You turn round and get a fright
Loads of bags in your face
Then you open your pencil case
You look at your timetable and guess what you see?
You're supposed to be in ICT
You stand where you are and get pushed about
Until the crowd has cleared out
You spit out your piece of gum
Then you decide to run
You are glad, you are glad you are not being pushed
Then the bell goes and you start to rush
You climb up the towering stairs

TRUTH

And you flick back your long hair
You think to yourself, why did you run...

Helena May Summers (11)
King Edward VI High School, Stafford

THE TRUTH ABOUT THE TREES

Truth

T he truth about the trees
H ere upon the silent woods
E dged up in the sky

T he trees that spread their arms so wide
R ight up to the clouds
U ngazed are their beloved leaves
T hat reach high and low
H ow the leaves spread is unbelievable

A fter time the leaves all fall
B ut at this time it is so beautiful
O n the leaves the children play
U nder the leaves the dogs will stay
T ill the cold, dark night

T o this comes the fresh new leaves
H ow they glow and shine
E ach and every one is different

TRUTH

T o this the trees look beautiful

R ight over again

E very year the same thing happens

E ach and every year

S o we say this happy poem for the world to hear.

Phoebe Rose Unwin (11)
King Edward VI High School, Stafford

LIFE AND DEATH

Truth

Everyone fears death because it's painful
But life is more painful than death
Maybe it's because they know death is the truth
And life is just a lie you live every day

In life you change yourself to fit in
You get hurt every day
But when you die you are free to be yourself forever
Without anyone judging you and you are free from pain

Death is and always will be in your pocket following you
Everywhere and every day
Until one day you ask, 'When will you be coming?'
But death will say, 'You're not ready yet.'
So you live on knowing you are living in a world
Full of lies and pain

But sometimes life can be beautiful
You have your friends and family
The loving nature around you
Then you realise you never want to leave.

Katie Leavy
King Edward VI High School, Stafford

TRUTH

MY LITTLE MONSTER

Truth

My life is different to yours
We have a little creature with paws who also roars

Sometimes he will beg for food
But that's because he wants a walk

When he is on a walk he normally gives up
But that's normal because he's done that since he was a pup

Freddie will never ignore a treat
Especially if it is meat

At times he will think he's more important than me
But I know that's not true because I'm the owner you see

He can read my mood whether I'm happy or sad
As he never wants my day to be bad

He hates going to the vets
Even though that's where you take all the pets

There's nothing that can replace my dog
Although I do wonder what it would be like to have a frog.

Ella Castree-Denton (11)
King Edward VI High School, Stafford

TRUTH

POEM ABOUT THE TRUTH

Truth

The sun is shining
I'm still growing
My friends are smiling
And the day is going

Writing this song where I belong
Knowing right from wrong where I'm strong
All along I long for your song
Mentally playing ping-pong moving along all along

Horsing around
Head towards the ground
Making no sound
Feeling homebound
Feeling lost but not found

Smoke in the air
No sigh of despair
Turn it down just a hair
People watch and stare
But, I don't mean to scare
Playing truth or dare
Repairing my tear... preparing my flare

TRUTH

THE POETRY GAMES: TRUTH OR DARE? - VOICES FROM THE
MIDLANDS

Banging this gong... of waiting to belong
Writing this song... not knowing right from wrong

I have no urge to weep
I have no time to sleep.

Mia Hewison (13) & Tyler Oxley Wheeler
King Edward VI High School, Stafford

PRAY FOR SYRIA

Truth

Several thousand people stranded from their homes
Waiting for news about their country
Trying to get abroad to safety
Hoping they will stay alive

Young children terrified about what is going on
Drowning while on safety boats
Displaced from their parents or homes
Being killed for no reason

Refugees flee to Europe
Sailing across the Mediterranean Sea
To safe countries, like Greece and Germany
Overwhelming their governments

ISIS destroying the nation of Syria
USA and Russia working together to kill them
Terrorising Iraq as well
Destroying cities, town and villages

A nation with such beauty
A nation which was safe before
Every single nation is supporting
Everyone, pray for Syria.

Thomas Fox (11)
King Edward VI High School, Stafford

TRUTH

MY DAD AND ME

Truth

My dad was a very nice dad
He was a little naughty
But he wasn't that bad
Me and my dad have lots of memories

My memories with my dad
Are my treasure, always will be
None of them are bad
You will like my dad, just wait and see

I love my dad
I always have
Sometimes I get a bit sad
My dad passed away sadly

If I could write a million pages about him
I would still be unable to say
Just how much I love and miss him
Every single day

Sometimes I would call him
While I was doing my homework
If I got stuck he would help me
Through all of the problems
He would tell me the answers
But I love him because he is my dad.

Amber Wilson (11)
King Edward VI High School, Stafford

TRUTH

THE WORDS THAT THEY SAY

Dare

The words that they say still etched into my mind
I've lost count of how many times I've cried
There's no barrier between thoughts and feelings
Why are people so mean? After all, we are all human beings
So I've come to the conclusion that I have no meaning

People never stop until it's too late
They never stop spreading hate
They only realise they've gone too far
When they see the hearse from afar

Wanting the pain to end
Thinking that you have no friends
Feeling vulnerable, unwanted and useless
You think the only option is to end this
So when the final curtains are drawn
You know you can't go back to way it was before.

Emily Harris (14) & Ottie
King Edward VI High School, Stafford

DARE

THE RAILWAY MEN

Truth

Faster than horses, faster than birds whistling through the
countryside
With coaches or freights bursting through stations
Shunting in yards
This is the age of the railway man
Pushing coaches into the station, preparing the freight
Shunting the brake van and pulling a rake
Eating a sandwich while watching the trains
Watching the might of a train pulling a rake
This is the age of the railway man
Pulling into the station to board, to embark
Pulling out the station with gushes of steam
Over the hills and over the lake into the tunnel and onto the
bridge
Up the embankment and into the yard, back to the sheds to
park and depart
This is the age of the railway man.

Barney Brass (13)
King Edward VI High School, Stafford

TRUTH

WOLVERHAMPTON

Truth

W onderful
O verwhelming
L ovely
V ast
E xtraordinary
R espectful
H omely
A ncient
M olineux
P erfect
T ough
O utstanding
N ice

Wolverhampton is a fantastic place
Sometimes it's overwhelming
The people are lovely
In this extraordinary place
And always make you welcome

When you're tired and just wanna chill
Make sure you visit the Holcombe Hotel
You can go by car or even train
Just make sure you dodge the rain

TRUTH

Speaking about weather
Don't complain
The Wolverhampton lot are as hard as nails!

Henry Price (11)
King Edward VI High School, Stafford

LIFE IS TOO SHORT

Dare

Life can be good
Life can be bad
Even though it's bad
You need to make the most of it

Sometimes it can be amazing
Sometimes it isn't great
But life is too short
And you need to make the most of it

Living life to the full
It is such an amazing experience
Having a good time
And reaching the highest heights
Life will be enjoyable

Sometimes life can be good
Sometimes life can be bad
It is just too short
And you need to make the most of it

Although life can be bad sometimes
You need to think about the positives
And on the bright side
You just have to.

Christopher Austin
King Edward VI High School, Stafford

DARE

LA OLYMPICS 2018

Truth

LA, the beautiful city
Hosting the 2028 Olympics
I think it will be terrific
But it will be a pity if I can't be there

How I would love to see the races
With all the cheers and happy faces
If I could race my hero Andre De Grasse
Then I will be happy as I am racing someone fast

I love doing sport
That's why I aim to be there
But I have to work hard at it because I really care

Now I've reached it I'm finally there
On the track, no looking back
Looking forwards to the race
I hope I can keep up the pace
And finish this Olympic race.

Christopher Arthur (11)
King Edward VI High School, Stafford

TRUTH

FLORA AND FAUNA

Dare

Nature, you help mankind in ways we can't begin to describe
The way you purify the air of our sins and crimes
We owe so much to you, nature, that I decided to praise you in rhyme
Oh flora, how you absorb the light to conceive the air we breathe,
Oh how you provide shelter to us as the rain pours down
Or how you decorate our gardens with your beauty when we begin to frown
Oh fauna, how you disperse the plants' seed around the globe we call Earth
Oh ocean, how you and your water provides nourishment and pleasure to our lives
Oh what would we do without you nature by our sides?

Harvey Bridgeman
King Edward VI High School, Stafford

DARE

WHAT OCTOBER 2017 MEANS TO ME...

Truth

It's the month of October
And my sister's baby's due
Evenings are getting colder
Dinners are mainly stew

I can't wait to be an uncle
To little baby Rosie
It will be nice to give her a cuddle
With my present, a cuddly pony

Conkers and leaves are falling
A sign of winter too
Nearly time for Christmas shopping
Halloween and Bonfire Night first in the queue

Halloween is on the thirty-first
Waiting all month is the worst
All us children trick or treating
Eating too many sweets and ready to burst.

Ryan Benjamin Frost (11)
King Edward VI High School, Stafford

TRUTH

HOMELESS

Truth

You see them at night cross-legged on the floor
Begging for money or food or even more
They have no idea when they will next eat
So why don't they try another street?

They have nowhere to go or even hide
They think everyone is on the opposite side
You could give them a chance, or walk on by
But they're used to this, so they probably won't cry

When you're at home, enjoying the heat
Think about these guys lying cold in the damp, wet street
Next time you see them take a step back
Buy them a sandwich and stop for a chat.

Lucas Willson (11)
King Edward VI High School, Stafford

TRUTH

THE SECRET

Dare

In the back of my head it dwells
An unholy thought that lies in slumber
This secret, too violent to tell
So big it was now a cumber

It whispers and scratches at the walls
The ache and thought of hell
The secret so deeply buried, it now creeps and calls
This secret I wish to dispel;

But there's just one problem
I can't escape
This secret made me numb
But now it's time to make a break

I'll tell you my secret of sorrow and despair
My mouth opens but nothing comes out, nothing but cold,
sharp air...

Nico Anderson (15)
King Edward VI High School, Stafford

THE SCHOOL YEAR

Truth

The holidays are over
The school year has begun
What will happen
Will it be fun?

Will I get an iPad?
Will I get a phone?
No probably not
I'm as lazy as a bone

Will I play hockey?
Will I win a race?
Will I score a goal?
That would be ace

Will I do a club?
Which will it be?
Maybe rugby
I'll have to wait and see

What will it be like?
To be in Year Seven
Will it be like hell?
Or will it be like heaven?

Daniel Bennett (11)
King Edward VI High School, Stafford

TRUTH

WHY?

Dare

Why is the world so cruel?
Why do people fight?
Why do children have to see their families destroyed?
Why is this still happening?

Why are people so cruel?
Why do people call each other names?
Why, when under our own skin, we are the same?
Why is this still happening?

Why is everything so expensive?
Why do people have to struggle so much?
Why are so many people homeless?
Why is this still happening?

Why? Why? Why?

Chloe Deakin (11)
King Edward VI High School, Stafford

EXAMS

Truth

Exams! Exams! Exams! That's all I hear
Revise this, revise that, learn this and learn that
Maths, English, science galore
History, geography, RE and more
Two years to go till the time is here
I'm already stressing and it's not even near
Revision, sleep, revision, sleep
Books and paper scattered in a heap
Tired already but I must go on
Lots to do, before time has gone
My heart is racing, how can this be done?
I'll do my best, then I can have fun.

Bethany Clinton
King Edward VI High School, Stafford

DARE WE BE OURSELVES?

Truth

Dare we speak our minds
At the risk of being judged?
Dare we be a judge of others
At the risk of being singled out?
Dare we be ourselves
At the risk of not fitting in?
Dare we not fit in
At the risk of being called a loner?
Dare we be a loner
At the risk of being bullied?
To prove that they're wrong
Dare we seek help from others
At the risk of looking weak?
Dare we look weak
When help is all we seek?

Max Elkin
King Edward VI High School, Stafford

TRUTH

MYSELF

Truth

My name is Reece, I like to keep the peace
I go to the Fight Factory
I like to keep smart
I like to look the part
My GI is the key
I focus on the fights
I try to get it right
It's about taking part, being a team player
I never lose heart
I'm a winner because I believe in myself
I fight for my goals, medals hanging on my wall
Trophy after trophy
The best thing I could ever achieve is continuing being me.

Reece Sutherland (11)
King Edward VI High School, Stafford

TRUTH

SOCIETY

Dare

Stop!
If you come to my city you will run for the hills
It's too populated
Too much congestion
Time for a change
Time to stand out
Let's stop congestion
Let's get out
Let's change your society for the greater good
And look forward to the future
Let's not let our society crumble into dust
And get blown away
Stand up, shout out and rebuild our city
Are you with us?

Adam (13) & Christian Robinson (13)
King Edward VI High School, Stafford

12AM

Truth

I can't sleep
My thoughts are too deep
I watch the sky
The peaceful streets
I sing to the moon
Humming a random tune
As the people around me dream
I sit and think
As the tears start to fall
Running down my face
I push my thoughts aside
As I climb into bed
Hoping I will be able to fall asleep
And I go
Until I'm awoken by the same dream that haunted me
before.

Jessica Martin
King Edward VI High School, Stafford

TRUTH

THE POETRY COMPETITION

Truth

Busy day at school
Trying to ignore some fool
The walk home, take a while
Talking to a friend about his new hairstyle
Arrive home, but hell's not ended
I have poetry homework, splendid
Stressing, struggling
Until finally, after hours of messing
My dad says to me,
'Why not write about the poetry competition?'
So I say, 'OK.'
And I do.

Morgan Steventon (11)
King Edward VI High School, Stafford

TRUTH

PRESIDENT NOW

Truth

Donald Trump is the president now
Most of us thought, *oh wow, how?*
He's picking a fight with Kim Jong-un
Neither will back down until damage is done
They're spitting and shouting and baring their teeth
Which one will be first to lay a wreath?
Left much longer, it'll be too late to mend
Who on earth knows where this will end?

Jacob Murray (15)
King Edward VI High School, Stafford

TRUTH

RACISM

Dare

Black and white
They are the same
No different
Treat them the same
You all get on the same train
They should all get paid the same
Why should you judge by their colour?
One is equal to another
This is because of the past
People are killing one another
This is so wrong
Stop it now.

Hayden Burrows (14)
King Edward VI High School, Stafford

COOKING

Truth

C oriander is added to the stock

O il is heated

O nly one inch above in the pan goes the oil

K now when to add turmeric, ginger, garlic

I n the pan goes the salt and pepper

N ow add lime juice

G arlic and ginger rice is what you have.

Elijah Hayes (11)
King Edward VI High School, Stafford

TRUTH

BROKEN-HEARTED

Truth

I remember the day we first met
I remember the day we went out
I remember the love we had, I remember the love that I had
for you
I hated that we always had a fight
I hated to see you leave
I remember the fun times we had
I remember the night I snuck out to see you
I used to hate the wars we would start
I used to hate to hear you say goodbye
I look back to what we had; the strong bond for each other
I look at myself now and I see a weak and useless person
All I feel now is pain, the pain from my broken heart from
when you left me

I miss you, I miss you... I'd give anything to see you again
I would give my life to be with you again
But in the end I can't live without you my love, so these are
my final words to you
Follow your heart, don't overtake it
If you leave it behind, someone will break it
Goodbye...

Aron John Brydon (14)

Lincoln University Technical College, Lincoln

TRUTH

RAP

Truth

People say that music never helps
That it makes you lose concentration
And that the artists can influence you to do bad things
That rap is the worst
But at the end of the day
Rap is just a poem

But to me it is more than just a poem
Rap helps me a lot
To concentrate
To be calm
To be happy
And to feel relieved

The more I listen to rap
The more I feel that weight drops off my shoulders
And the more I can concentrate
On the road ahead
The couplets, the metaphors, the adjectives, the alliteration
And finally
The poems

I can concentrate on it all
When I listen to rap
My imagination becomes my life

TRUTH

My road ahead
Becomes clear
With no more burden on my shoulders

I can write creative stories
Poems and novels
It all spills out
When I concentrate with my rap
And I do the best work I can
To the best of my ability

But at the end of the day
People say music never helps
But it helps people in different ways
And at the end of the day
Poems are just raps

The things we have to learn for our GCSEs
The hours spent studying
Learning, revising and remembering
And in the end we get a piece of paper
That tells us how good we are
How good we can be

And all we need to do
Is concentrate
And do our best
Then we can relax
Listen to some rap

TRUTH

And be
Proud, relieved and maybe even daydream

Because the troubles are over
No more studying or revising
Learning or remembering
You can finally be free to live your life
And be who you want to be

To see the jobs you can get
For me
Rap has helped me get this far
Without rap I would not be doing my best
But rap has helped me to reach success

And not to be afraid
To do my best
To be who I want to be
To live my life how I want to
With no rules
Or people telling me what to do.

Ethan Ward
Lincoln University Technical College, Lincoln

TRUTH

DAD

Truth

Why?
Why did the world take you away?
Why did it take you away before I could make memories?
Why the heartbreak and the tears?

Dad
From what I have been told
You were smart and kind
You were caring and athletic
You were courageous and funny
You helped a lot of people
You were an honourable man

Memories
I can only recall some vague memories
Like the time the bird landed on your head
Like the time we went to the tram museum
The only other way I remember is the photos and the stories
The last thing I remember is sitting next to you in your
hospital bed eating your wine gums

I miss you so much and would do anything to get more time
with you and more memories
Nothing could buy the memories back and you can't buy
back all the time I've lost without you.

Jack Armitage (14)
Lincoln University Technical College, Lincoln

TRUTH

CORRUPTION

Dare

Corruption - the understanding of this word is pretty much misunderstood
EU, the Americas and Asia: the list goes on of countries trying to lead your understanding
Wrong or right that's up to you but personally it's wrong, how can a government change you?
Overseas, it's where it's all kicking off, a nuclear holocaust brewing as we speak
Why does no one say anything about the tragedies that happened
Less than 100 years ago?
Gas! Gas! No more
But now even worse people have moved on, discoveries helped, or have they?
You see, back to our home - the place we call safe, the people we trust

Influencing us like we're robots; this is the future pretty much in a nutshell
Turn on your TV
What you see we all take for candour - supposedly true is it though?
How? How can we assume the facts
Drilled into us daily
No treatment for illness
Lies

DARE

Make America great again - ha
It should have been, let's screw our country up
Makes me laugh really
You gave stick to the old leader - now you wish you hadn't
Props to him; he did a better job
Leaving the EU that's all anyone talks about, but is that really the biggest problem?
Go to the coast, go look at the amazement that is the plastic whale for all to see
But no one pays attention - maybe for a few days, a week at most
Just like this poem - a few moments later gone, out of sight, out of mind
Go see a dolphin. Take a selfie. Why not kill it while you're at it?
Money makes the world go round
A simple piece of cotton; fabric-like
Like humans, they have a price
All have a different value and a different place holder
It's all good - put your faith in an invisible being
I mean let's have an opinion; let's speak what we think. Why should we keep quiet?
Why should we not be able to address what we think is right and wrong?
To me this is the definition of corruption.

Regan King (14)
Lincoln University Technical College, Lincoln

BULLIED

Dare

She is crying at school, you call her weak
What you don't know is:
Her mum could die
Her dad is depressed
Her brother needs therapy and she just can't help

She takes a knife and cuts her arms
She takes unnecessary pills
Even her 'friends' have blocked her out
She doesn't come to school today, you think she is pathetic

What you don't know is:
Her mum passed away last night
Her dad has turned to alcohol
Her brother ran away and she wants to take her own life
She takes a knife once more and takes those pills again

A week later, there is an announcement on the intercom
The girl you bullied has died
She committed suicide last night
At first you don't care
At first you find it funny
What you don't know is:
It was her mum's funeral two days before
She didn't go
Guilt-ridden - she wished she did

DARE

Her brother had been missing for a week
She loved him dearly
Her dad became abusive
She thought he was her hero
She picked up that knife for the final time and took those
pills for the final time

Her brother saw the headlines, he came home just for her,
and now he is depressed

It came to the day
The day of her funeral
Everyone went
Her dad and her brother too

You, the one who bullied her for 'being weak' realise what
you made her do
You wish you could speak to her for just one second, you
wish you could say you're sorry
You want her to know
You need her to know
You wish you could turn back the clocks to the day she was
crying at school
You realise what you need to do
There are people to stop you
She felt like she had no one
Don't be too quick to judge
You don't know what goes on behind closed doors

Imagine if the roles were reversed
How would you cope?

Nicole Scrupps (14)

Lincoln University Technical College, Lincoln

DARE

THAT NIGHT

Truth

That night screaming was heard from the graveyard
Then I started hearing voices so I got ready to strike hard
Swings creaking with the aggressive breeze from the west
After what I've witnessed I believe I would not get rest
Me and Ewan ran to the nearest sight of light
To only wait round the corner to find quite the fright
A shadow formed from the corner in the shape of a man
Noises came from the road sounding like a van
It pulled up behind us, we did not know what to do
Besides run for our life from what we knew we might not
pull through
We started to head back to mine, cutting through all fields
Picking up everything which can be used as shields
We were right outside mine ready to jump through the door
My mum asked us if we were alright, we did not respond
and fell to the floor.

Jack Hatcher (14)

Lincoln University Technical College, Lincoln

THE LIE WE LIVE

Truth

I would like to tell you what the problems in the world are today
The world today has many problems with politics and the way we live
Every morning you wake up to go to school or go to work, all up until you retire and then... death
You see we live in a world where everyone is money-hungry, homeless people left to starve and we do nothing about it
See money exists because someone needs something more than the other
But if we continue this the results will be critical
More and more people will become homeless and the death rates will increase
So many politicians, the world is now falling into corruption

We are like the slaves of the world working for the government
Building their buildings and letting them make more money and most of our lives being forced to work for money to stay alive, until we die
We never get the chance to fully enjoy living

We choose our leaders of the country by voting and they decide what we do and how we live
Which should never be the case, it makes life very boring not being able to live life to the fullest

TRUTH

Companies are making money from our health
which is truly disgusting
If you have cancer and no money then you get no health
care, which is horrible, really horrible
We really need to make a revolution,
sure we have improved health care but only for people who
have money
which is why deaths are becoming more frequent and that
cancer is now taking over

So many trees being cut down that the future will have no
nature to see and it will be devastating
So many species of animals will become extinct
and the future generations will no longer be able to see
them
We all need to stand together and help the world as a
whole,
no more wars and let's all be together as one
I am no poet artist but I made this to make people realise
the 'lie we live'
So let's enjoy the life of living!

Leon Jake Goodhew (14)
Lincoln University Technical College, Lincoln

FIRST WORLD PROBLEMS

Dare

So, you're British: a quintessentially posh stereotype, yes?
No. Because the picture on the streets is looking a lot less
'Leonardo da Vinci' and a lot more bleak
See that tap over there with an uncontrollable leak?
You may as well be burning money - what's that? The Tories
did? It wouldn't surprise me
Because all they like to do is balance bills on the back of you
Until
Your
Back
Breaks
And they pick a new victim to torment with debt...

Debt... it's not a nice feeling when your bank balance sinks
below the point of no return;
When the bailiffs start knocking at your door til you don't
have one anymore.
Nobody has an escape, for that matter.
The ones who can reach their exits are at the top of
their ivory towers
Or sat in the Houses of Parliament, debating whether they
should give junior doctors
Their rights
Or just punish them for their strikes

DARE

By making them responsible for dressing the wound of a
broken NHS
While thousands are denied a hospital bed

But politicians are deaf to the hoots of the working class
From their second mansions up on cloud nine
While everyone else works nine to five keeping them up
there.

Then again, it could be worse
You could be in America while being not white, female and
anything but straight.
Want to get over the border?
If your name sounds Muslim, you'll have to wait.
All this coming from a man who hates foreigners but has a
foreign wife...
Hypocrisy? I think so.
But why is the Earth spinning backwards to fuel Donald
Trump's ego?
Oh, and one more cheerful thought before you go:
The impending possibility of WW3.

Alexandra Senkiw-Smith (14)
Lincoln University Technical College, Lincoln

PERFECTION

Truth

Perfection
Who makes up such a word?
An unattainable goal
An ideal that can drown you
In an ocean of pain
Is it worth the pain?
Is it worth the pain to still never be good enough?
Is it worth the pain just to make yourself more imperfect?
Is it worth the trauma to just be reduced to tears over and
over and over again?
So why do we push it?
Why exactly do we
Pressure others to change?
To starve their bodies
To cry
To scar their porcelain skin?

Perfection
Another crazy proposal
Another way to crush our spirits
'You're fat'
'You're ugly'
'You're useless'
But if we can't be perfect then what is our purpose?
No one wants anything less

TRUTH

Useless
Ugly
Stupid
Just words to cause pain
Words we use to describe ourselves
When we're feeling low
When we're feeling blue
When we just don't know what to do

But when there is no escape
When there is no one there
What if we want it all to end
But don't even have the courage to tell anyone we're
hurting
And just keep it locked up inside
A time bomb ready to blow
But when it blows
What will we do?
End everything
All the pain and misfortune?
Or end ourselves
Take away our suffering
But leave more pain in our wake?
Or stay
And try oh so hard to just keep going
And not give up
And stay strong
And not take our one and only life away?

TRUTH

But I ask
Perfection
Is it really worth it?

Kati Louise Robinson (15)

Lincoln University Technical College, Lincoln

TRUTH

THE DRAWER

Truth

There is always that drawer
That always seems to store
His useless things that accumulate
Whether it's crap or whether it's great

It's never meant to be there
It appears from thin air
From the old torch
Or the bread that was scorched

Maybe a wad of blue tack
Even a piece of train track
The one battery left in the pack
Also a squeaky duck going quack

There is loose change
A puzzle you can never arrange
Fragments of a pen
Or even an incomplete model Mercedes-Benz

All in all there are things that are left
You'd maybe assumed it was theft
The things that were forgotten
Like a ball of yarn or cotton

This was like nothing I ever saw
This, my friend, is the drawer.

Ben Rodgers (14)
Lincoln University Technical College, Lincoln

TRUTH

MY NAN

Truth

Although we didn't have the best relationship,
It was hard to see it through,
And those few years she was ill,
Our relationship grew and grew.

It started as a common cold, my grandad had it too,
But it clung to her chest, every day it wasn't something
brand new,
She got more ill by the second,
No one knew what to do,
So she visited the doctor and he said she had the flu,
But there was still one more option,
It could be a tumour too.

She wandered off to the hospital scared what the doctors
would say,
She found out she had cancer and it was spreading each
and every day,
They treated it like normal,
But yet it wasn't working,
She was old and frail,
And her lungs weren't supporting,
It had gone too far,
Her lungs had to be drained,
From the fluid left inside of her,
That had yet attacked in vain.

TRUTH

She got more ill each day, there was nothing we could do,
She ended up in hospital and we thought she wouldn't see it
through,
But in a few weeks, when she headed home in a wheelchair,
Everything was back to brand new,
When she couldn't do much her spirit was high,
But we knew we didn't have much time left,
That her ending was nigh.

On the 21st of December 2015,
She fluttered her wings and flew away,
Time goes slowly when one is passing,
And my nan in a coffin she will lay.

Paris Jessie Layzell (14)
Lincoln University Technical College, Lincoln

CORRUPTION OF SCHOOL

Dare

Your Honour, I would like to put the Department of
Education on trial because
In school we are taught one way no matter what, yet each
kid is different
The schools teach everyone exactly the same, yet some kids
need different help or no help at all
Each kid has different idea, abilities and more, yet it's the
same
We are asked why we were all doing so badly in exams and
teachers wonder why
It's because each and every kid is taught the same
Schools are killing our creativity
When schools were first started we were taught one way
and that was to program us to work in factories
That was over 150 years ago
Yet this is the present, yet we are still being taught the same
way as we were all those years ago
And we wonder why each generation turns out to be like
robots
It's because each school teaches kids the same, it's the
murder of our creativity
So today, Your Honour, I would like to call the Department
of Education up to the stand for the murder of today's kids'
creativity

DARE

As we see in classrooms the placing are set out in rows and
columns, just like in factories
A goldfish can be related to the same system, when
programmed one way it can only do what it is taught
Yet when given freedom and creativity it is able to find new
things and new ways in its life
The Department of Eduction is killing the creativity and
uniqueness in kids
So, Your Honour, I rest my case.

Shaun Cozens (14)
Lincoln University Technical College, Lincoln

LOVE LIKE COFFEE

Truth

You're the heat to my boil
You're the sweet to my sugar
You're the cream to my milk
You're the energy to my caffeine
You're the bitterness to my grains
You're the love to my life
But
Eventually the boil stops
The water cools
The sugar dissolved
The milk goes sour
The rush of energy ends
The bitterness lingers

Now you're gone, far away
And
Across the oceans, I travel to you
A mission I deliver, to make immense
The hours pass by till I knock on your door
I stand. Waiting

The door finally open, my heart beats fast
Then
Seeing you for the first time
I take in every detail of your pale face

I feel myself go bright red realising
I fell in love once again
I regather my thoughts
Deep breath

I try to apologise and you shut me out
Until it is this poem that I recite
I see a faint silhouette walk towards the door
It opens and I fall silent as a tear drops
There's a spark and a click
Suddenly

The kettle's switch flicks and it boils again
A new cup is presented
The sugar re-added
Milk renewed
The grains of caffeine back again
And now I present to you
The perfect cup of coffee.

Grace Harley (14)
Lincoln University Technical College, Lincoln

ME

Truth

I want the this
I want the that
I hate the this
I hate the that

Do I?
Do I?

Every day I stay the same
Never question what I cannot tame:
The anger, the fear, why I don't even have gear

'No pain, no gain.'
It was me to blame

I want the this
I want the that
I hate the this
I hate the that

No
No I don't

I was trapped inside a cage
By a something
I don't really know what it was
Me, the Wizard of Oz?

TRUTH

That doesn't really matter to me
The fact was it was a plague to me
Stopping me from being myself you see

I don't want the this
I don't want the that
I don't hate the this
I don't hate the that

Materials! Materials! Get your materials!
Sorry, I won't make my own burial
I have no such desires
I refuse to rest on my funeral pyre

I understand now
All things negative about me are a result of me
It just hit me like pow!
And finally, I understood who I must be

Quite simply, me.

Mark Bradshaw (14)
Lincoln University Technical College, Lincoln

GOODBYE SOCIETY

Dare

Society, society
We forgot about society
But it doesn't matter as long as we got our salary
Remember last week? When we saw that man die
But what did we do, oh yeah, we turned a blind eye
We saw that one good cop, he seemed like a nice guy
Then why is it he ignored all that she said
When she came in crying after being forced into someone else's bed?

Society, society
Oh what happened to society?
'Cause we keep pushing people away and triggered the anxiety
Remember just yesterday when you were being a cheat
And saw that young woman dragging her kid along the street?
Well guess what; every night that poor child gets beaten
The lonely kid, only aged three
Got nobody to listen to his silent plea

Society, society
We screwed up society
I guess we should've held on to our sanity
But instead we just walked away from it at a steady pace
With all those warm tears running down your face

DARE

No wonder your momma called you a disgrace
So please tell me what it is that happened to society
Can we all please take back our God-damned humanity?

Rachel Odlin (14)

Lincoln University Technical College, Lincoln

NO REGRETS

Dare

If I want to I can look back
And say I should have done this or that
But I don't
And if I want to I can look back
And say I take back this or that
But I don't
And even though I am far from a perfectionist
I think that everything I have done has gone as perfectly as I
wish
Because it has
Every backfiring joke, every time I spoke
Out of turn is a wonder to me
And every mistake I make and risk I take and time I was late
Brings me closer to being complete
And while I feel there's a time
Where I stepped out of line
And someone tried to send me a sign
That I did something that didn't turn out fine
For every friend I left behind
And each little thing I have yet to find
Which means I just have to try better next time
So can you say that this is a crime?
That I want to improve on my own mind
Because it's not

DARE

And while you may think I am stupid for saying this
If I could go back
And try to do this or that
I wouldn't change a thing
I'm stating a fact
Because I wouldn't have it any other way.

Ben Edward Davis (15)

Lincoln University Technical College, Lincoln

THRILLS

Dare

Drugs, they're only things for thugs
Already your grave's being dug
And for all you gangstas
To you nothing matters
Soon you'll be dying
And leaving your family crying
Here you are sticking the needle in
After that you passed out in a bin
Wake up craving, eating moss
'Cause you're high off your head and don't give a toss
You all think you're a boss man
'Cause you drive around in your transit van
Full substances that have been banned
Going to make yourself a millionaire man
Hiding all this from your parents
And even your old, weak grandparents
Imagine what they'd think
If they saw you sat there on the brink
Watching you constantly sink
Into hallucination
Of pure fascination
Your family carrying your coffin
Thinking you could have been a boffin

DARE

Whoever got you in can't get you out
And you'll soon become a sprout
Reborn and let out.

Callum Benfield (14)
Lincoln University Technical College, Lincoln

THE STARS

Truth

He came home one night
And then we went outside
The stars were out shining nice and bright
He took my hand and led me in
We asked the question and got the answer we needed

We put on our winter coats
And wrapped up warm
So we stepped out the house
And I squeezed his hand
Then and there I knew, no harm could come to me

The moon was out
Along with the stars
And he spun me around and looked me up and down
All he did was bite his lip

A single word changed everything
Even the stars lit up
All he said was, 'Wow,' and my face started to hurt
That smile of his made everything clear, I am his and he is
mine

Then that night I slept easy
With my baby by my side

TRUTH

Not a single drop of sadness came rolling out my eyes
Another night made perfect by my special baby.

Georgia Stevenson (14)
Lincoln University Technical College, Lincoln

A WORLD MADE OF PLASTIC

Dare

Seagulls aren't flying
Fish are dying
Whales made of plastic
This occurrence is drastic
How can people be so careless?

Fish are like they are made out of plastic
Recycling is all it takes just to save a precious life
The life of the ocean world is slowly dying, turning to an afterlife
If we don't act fast, the world we once knew, gone forever

The world is slowly dying
Dying till there's nothing left
What will we do then?
When our world has gone due to our careless actions

What will we do then?
When we have nowhere to live
Nowhere to eat or drink
If our world goes, we go
When you have finished a bottle, just stop and think
What will this do to our planet?
Put it in the recycling

DARE

Only then can you have our precious planet and save
thousands of lives.

Edward Ruddock (14)
Lincoln University Technical College, Lincoln

BE GOOD

Dare

How much money is spent
On the environment?
Not enough, that's what
All these animals get shot
All these trees chopped
And all for what?

Money and riches all your heart can desire
Just ignore that forest fire
Inside their rooms children play
While the planet continues its decay
The society we live in is beginning to fray
Yet almost no one is in dismay

The ones ruling the world
Have heads filled with mould
Off the missiles go
Pull the pin and throw
'You've been shot!'
'I know.'
No one has love left to show

We're all gonna die eventually
So live your life successfully
Save the trees
Look after the bees

DARE

Be kind and care like you should
Be good.

Spencer Beeson (14)

Lincoln University Technical College, Lincoln

FAMILY

Truth

Our family are who we love and who we stick with
They stick with us through thick and thin

I would help them do a lot of things
Like taking the trash out to the bin

My mum, my dad, my sister
All a part of me and my family

From dusk till dawn I stay with them
Like when we went camping and made a den

This family was like a maze and the look on my family's faces
Was like they had seen a dog in space

My family has much to learn
Like a crisp of fire, like burns

All my family were looking at me
Whilst I was sat at the table eating my tea
At this moment in time, I was dreaming of a paradise
When sitting with my family, watching the veritable nights go by.

Ethan Richardson (14)
Lincoln University Technical College, Lincoln

TRUTH

2017

Dare

First Trump was elected
Then we ended up paying for Brexit
Ballistic missiles flying across the skies
And Trump's trying to cover up his lies
One fired after another
Soon it'll be one war after another
While volcanoes erupt
Our leaders are getting more and more corrupt

Acid attacks
Terrorist attacks
489 injured and 59 dead because of one man
Cared about one day, forgotten the next
Gun and run like it's just for fun
North Korea still testing
Never resting, never ending
Three hurricanes, one week
Destruction by nature and humans

Meanwhile the Earth's being polluted
Wildfires, hurricanes, volcanos and cars
Just pushed to the side like everything else.

Luke Foster (14)
Lincoln University Technical College, Lincoln

NUCLEAR WAR

Dare

America's meant to be a place for all
But people say to Mexicans, 'There ain't no place for y'all.'
Nuclear warfare about to kick off, being discussed in a hall
Trump, golfing, trying to smash the ball

He doesn't care, only about his orange hair

Kim Jong-un declares war
His nuke's hotter than the Earth's core
Look high and low for
Nuclear war!

The US is provoking North Korea
Only a few months until they blow
Not talking about Kim Jong-un
I'm talking about the 'nuke'

The world's evolving, Donald doesn't care
He only cares about his orange hair!

Mitchell Mays (14)
Lincoln University Technical College, Lincoln

DARE

WHAT FOR?

Dare

What about the way teens are treated?
What about the way they wear their jumpers?
The jumpers; hooded and dark
The dark alley one may stand
A gang!
A gang...
They must be in a gang
What for?
Drugs, violence, anything negative we can think of
Conjuring ideas of the unfaithful truth
What about
What about this?
They're running from their peers
Peers...
You sit next to them in class
Talk about the most random crap
Yet they chase you around until you're in that alley
The alley, your home away from home
You stand there like a piece of dirt or that gangster you are
Why does it happen?
Exactly!
What for?

Siobhan Watson (15)

Lincoln University Technical College, Lincoln

DARE

THE TRUTH OF OUR YOUTH

Dare

We try to get the message straight that we are not bad
people
We try to tell you that we are smarter than you
And we don't want you to give us some money just for a fix

Why do you think this way of us?
Some of us just want peace between the youth and the
police
All you do is look down on us
And we don't want you to think that we hate you police

You don't realise how isolated you make us feel
All the hate and fear you give us
The thing is you make us feel like we are peeled
Your incompetence kills us
We just want you to understand
To understand...
The real truth of our youth.

Ryan Arnold (15)
Lincoln University Technical College, Lincoln

DARE

THE EFFECT OF MUSIC

Truth

It changes you
It helps you out too

It makes you feel happy
It helps you not to get snappy

The rhythm makes you want to dance
It keeps you in a trance and gives you a chance

The lyrics help you concentrate
They also help you to dedicate

Its flow gives you freedom
All the demons in your life, you don't need 'em
It will keep you up when you are down
It'll keep you going without a frown

It will help you in times of need
And your life, you will start to lead
It is music
This is its effect, it'll hit you like a brick!

Kyle Fox (14)
Lincoln University Technical College, Lincoln

VIOLENCE BEHIND CLOSED DOORS

Dare

Behind the closed doors
Underneath her perfect flaws
His hand on her face
Putting her in 'her place'
He pushes and pulls
And when she finally falls
He stands over her grinning
While she is crawling
Away...

Away from the place
Where he laughs in her face
Away from the fear
And the smell of his rotten beer
Away from where she screams
She wants to fulfil her dreams

She says to her daughter
It can be just you and me
And we can be free
Away from his crippling power
Where he can't hurt us
So our happiness may flower.

Eloise Winterflood (14)
Lincoln University Technical College, Lincoln

DARE

LONELY

Dare

We're like a lark
Marching in the dark
Left, left, left, right, left
An ambush on our men
My friends drop one by one
The number eighty-one
My commander's name
Ringing in my mind
Those words
Those codes
Left, left, left, right, left
Till the lights go out
Blind at light
Till the smoke goes out
Not a doubt
I lay a heavy load
The enemies' feet swift past my ears
Like the whisper
My daughter gave so crisper
Those memories never to be seen or heard again
Those liars
Our men's dears
Never to pour some more beers.

Ayrton Alan Rowley (14)
Lincoln University Technical College, Lincoln

BITTER PEACE

Truth

The moment everyone had been waiting for
A celebration for both the rich and the poor
The soaring white doves signalled it had ended
For a deep wound was finally mended

The end of a war that never should have been
The likes of which none would wish to have seen
The blood on the field stains the hands of all
But strength and valour keeps us from our fall

Conflict always begins in times of darkness
When hope is short, all are left helpless
And although it was over, problems still remained
For violence and hatred could not be contained.

Jordi Folland (15)
Lincoln University Technical College, Lincoln

TRUTH

PROBLEMS FROM A TO WHATEVER I GET UP TO

Dare

Altruistic leaders acting up, arguing
Brushing away the boring bruising battles
Couldn't care less 'bout the calamity they're causing
Don't they see the damage they're doing daily?

Ecstatic entrepreneurs eating away
At the wonderful, fantastic fun-filled world
Gargantuan, greedy corporate businesses
Heating up the harmonious healthy Earth

Indolent, indecent, idle adolescences
Junkies, jokers, jacked up whacked up performers
Kids ignoring the kindred open-hearted
Brought up on lies, deceiving lyrics and loathing.

Liam Parks (15)
Lincoln University Technical College, Lincoln

DARE

SHARDS OF GLASS

Dare

How can people be so careless?
Put yourself in their shoes
Do you think they deserve this?

Think before you act
Not everyone's the same
Nobody is perfect
Nobody

How a heart can suddenly stop
And shatter into a million pieces
Once it is said
It never gets out my head

No one deserves to be called names
People are glass
They are fragile and can suddenly break

It doesn't matter how I look
How I act
This is me and no one can change that.

Clio Mackay (14)
Lincoln University Technical College, Lincoln

DARE

NOTHING MORE

Dare

Guns, gunpowder, nothing more than wishes
Sneering and hisses, lives better wishing
Guns, gunpowder, gashes and grazes,
Raises an alarm which causes nothing more than harm
A burning fire, a fuel for rampage,
A combustion of gall all for a forsaken cause,
Nothing more than a deadly course
Nothing more than a hobby for some,
Nothing more than a job for some,
But nothing more than an issue for all
A hair trigger away, a craze for some days,
Nothing more than a law,
Nothing more than a forsaken cause.

Alex Castleman (15)

Lincoln University Technical College, Lincoln

MURDER

Dare

It's the annihilation
The dismembering and insane temptation
That has got my concentration being in the state of
expatriation
It's the conjugation
Conjugation of a cleaver joining with the protoplasm
Causing a spasm of maximum satisfaction

It's the massacring
The smashing, slashing and thrashing
That has got my concentration in the state of bashing
It's the massacring
The massacring that is stopping their cardiovascular system
Beating the victim, erasing them from existence.

Paulius Rimkus (14)
Lincoln University Technical College, Lincoln

DARE

ELI

Truth

My little brother, only two
My little brother nothing to do

My little brother, I'm nearly home
But when I get in, he looks so alone

My little brother, I'm always here
You can't really see me, there's nothing to fear

My little brother, old or young
We will always have lots of fun

My little brother, you look so cold
But there're so many pages you have to unfold

My little brother, my best friend
Why does life have to end?

Leo Johns-Wait (14)
Lincoln University Technical College, Lincoln

SHADOW

Dare

A shadow, it is black as night
Can be seen at day, not at night
It follows like a baby duck, won't leave your side no matter what
There can be two or more, or none at all
They can be on her or him, or anyone
But this one is my shadow, no matter what, it will be mine
Through bad or good, no matter what, it will stay with me
It is smooth and soft as the bed of the Earth
It can be big or small or skinny or fat, no matter, it is mine
It will be mine 'til the end of my days...

Leo Alexander Hodson (15)
Lincoln University Technical College, Lincoln

DARE

POETRY

Dare

What is the point of poetry
Why does it exist?
It's futile indeed
Or is it?
It's a way of expressing anger, frustration and misery
And sometimes happiness and love
But still it can be painful to read and understand
And so much effort to write
Where would the world be without poetry?
Wouldn't it be better if it didn't exist?
Why are poets so famous?
What did they do to help the world?
I hate poetry
Or do I? I kind of like this poem.

Joseph Ager (14)
Lincoln University Technical College, Lincoln

THE RELIEF

Truth

She played her arm like a violin
All the pain she was in
The scars on her hips
She can't help but think
Why am I here?
Look at the state I'm in
As the tears flow from her bloodshot eyes
She screams, 'Why, just why?'
The scars on her arms
The silver blades against her wrist
As her parents cried, 'Why, just why?'
The body of a loved daughter
Lay lifelessly on the cold, hard floor.

Saffron Hartley (15)
Lincoln University Technical College, Lincoln

TRUTH

POLITICS

Dare

Politics
Its power can change the world
Politics
It scares innocent citizens like me
Politics
Terror attacks, it kills people you see
Politics
Even the law does it too
Politics
Donald Trump doesn't like the North Koreans
Politics
Britain leaving the European Union
Politics
Our world is dying slowly but surely
From global warming it's burning slowly.

Brett Jordan MacDonald (14)
Lincoln University Technical College, Lincoln

WHY?

Truth

They asked me why I did it
I tell them I don't know why
I ask myself why did I do it
I tell myself I don't know
They tell me this is not the girl we used to know
I reply I know
But that girl is not here anymore

I was trapped
They tell me it is easy
I tell them it's not
They say they don't understand
I say neither do I.

Isabelle Hughes (14)
Lincoln University Technical College, Lincoln

TRUTH

IF YOU WANT TO SEE AN ALIEN

Dare

If you want to see an alien
Just go to school
They will be all over you
They're your teachers
That is why they're strange
Not anyone can be a teacher

They can say lies to look smart
They can do more than most
They can see your lies
They can shout so loud
They will make us learn
Even if we don't want to...

Austin Alexander Bridgman (15)
Lincoln University Technical College, Lincoln

ALL FOR WHAT?

Dare

Hate and anger
Flood the streets
Manic leaders feed us lies
'9/11 was an inside job'
'Global warming is a myth'
The people we trust
To run our countries
Lying, stealing
And even starting wars
And all for what?
All for nothing.

Cameron Young (14)

Lincoln University Technical College, Lincoln

DARE

MY DAD IS A SOLDIER

Dare

It sounds like the gunshot
It made me think about war
What happened to my dad
When he went to war
He had flashbacks
When he hears a bang
He is glad he's trying
He is my hero
My dad is a soldier
My family is glad
That we have him back.

Courtney Killingsworth (15)
Lincoln University Technical College, Lincoln

DARE

FAKE KINGDOM

Dare

The patronising way that
The make-up's painted on.
All of those lies
And your childhood gone.

The filters, the fixtures
The smoke and the mirrors
The hiding that's going on
So you think there's nothing wrong.

Miss America, Miss UK
Miss Perfect; not me
There's never any quote:
'Be happy who you are
Don't push your beauty far.'

The sinking feeling
When your glass shoe's shone.
The death of love
And the poison apple's gone.

The fun that you posted
The end of the road is
All the same place,
Addictive misery.

Myla Parsons-Smith (12)
Manor House School, Ashby-De-La-Zouch

DARE

IT MUST BE...

Truth

Crunching leaves all around
The ground filled with conkers around
Red, orange, yellow and brown are the colours all around
Country and town
It must be autumn, I can smell it in the air
It must be the sight of autumn

Wrap up warm, run to the woods
Look out for squirrels scampering up
I hear conkers falling on the ground
It must be the sound of autumn

I smell hot dogs, onions and food
I look out my window and it changed my mood
Colour, colour and more colour
Crash, pop, bang, in the air
Yippee! It's Bonfire Night, take care!
It must be the fun time of autumn
Winter is in the air, so whilst you can
Autumn dance
Shake, shake, shake your leafy branch today
Nature's blanket is on its way
The air changed, damp, cold and grey
It must be the smell of autumn.

Lucy Cockell (11)
Mount St Mary's College, Spinkhill

TRUTH

CORNWALL

Truth

M1, A42, M42, M5, I know I am going west
To a beautiful place where I have lots of fun that I think is
the best
Trevone Bay to be precise
And all the friends that join us agree that it's just so nice
As soon as I get there my body board is in hand and wetsuit
on
I hope the wind is up so the waves haven't gone
I pray the red flag isn't out
As I descend on the beach, 'It's not!' I shout
The water is cold, salty and rough but as soon as I am under
That's it, I'm on a wave and I'm known as rumbling thunder
Next adventure is biking on the camel trail
Racing my mum who I usually call a snail
The flow rider is the place I like to go
Where I practise my surfing but unfortunately I stay quite
low
The natural swimming pool with its beautiful surround of
slate
The rocks make awesome jumping platforms for me and my
mates
All this has made me hungry, there is only one thing left to
get
Off to Padstow for a Cornish pasty and then watch the
gorgeous sunset

TRUTH

M5, M42, A42, M1, I know I am going away
Till the next time I see you Trevone Bay.

Elliot Parker (11)
Mount St Mary's College, Spinkhill

DONALD TRUMP

Dare

There was once a man called Trump
Who wanted the world to be a dump
He wouldn't listen, talk or reflect
He surely was an elected grump

All his comments on Twitter
They were all just sour and bitter
Shouting, screaming and bullying
He became the world's biggest critter

Trump was elected off the back of guns
His win came from their funds
His stupid love of guns
Why not bake some buns?

Trump wants another world war
Desperate not to be seen as a bore
Trying to intimidate North Korea
Donald Trump won't last much more

The rest of the world won't take the bait
The American people must relate
Then once again, the United States will be great.

Jenson Cole (11)
Mount St Mary's College, Spinkhill

DARE

OUR WORLD

Truth

Our world is always changing
The news and politics trying to be engaging
But we need a leader to tell us the truth
We need a leader to negotiate a worldwide truce
No matter what your race is
You know our world is in pieces
We need to elect a leader who represents change
We need to elect a leader who is going to rearrange
We need to unite as humans
We need to start revolutions
So don't go without leaving your mark
Because if you don't you will be remembered for nothing but
your last remark
So don't leave your problems for the next generation
Because all you'll give them is more frustration
Just because you wanted to live in a united world.

Sam Stacey (11)
Mount St Mary's College, Spinkhill

DONALD TRUMP

Dare

D onald was born just after the war
O ut of New York City
N o one believed he would go so far
A lthough he was clever he was never pretty
L eft university with an economics degree
D etermined to be the best he could be

T hirty years later he was a billionaire
R unning the family firm
U nlimited
M oney was not enough, he really wanted fame
P olitics is how we know his name

Why people like him we can't really say...
But Donald Trump is now President of the USA.

Alex Jakeman (11)
Mount St Mary's College, Spinkhill

DARE

SPRING

Truth

Diamonds falling from the clear blue sky
Gracefully balanced on the petals of the vibrant purple
flowers
Then a sprinkle of glitter on the dazzling leaves
The sun shooting bullets of light, the wind stopped in silence
The trees gasped and whispered
The diamonds came to a stop, a magical, colourful arch
Peering from the glistening white clouds up in the clear blue
sky
The birds begin to sing heavenly and the trees dance
carelessly
The wildlife coming to spring, everyone around starts to sing
Dew settling on the branches of the trees
Next maybe we'll see some bears having tea.

Evie C Bounds (11)
Mount St Mary's College, Spinkhill

TRUTH

STARTING SCHOOL

Truth

I started at school, I was no fool
But needed to try to reach the sky!

I met new friends, drove the teachers round the bends
But we'll make amends and be friends.

Incredibly great, with my brand new mates.
We walked down to the astro gate,
To play footy, it was great!

It's French, Spanish, English and maths
Up to art, my very worst class!
But I will try really hard to get a merit card.

The four weeks have been great with me and my mates
The Mount makes it count
I have no doubt the year will be great!

Luigi Lancaster-Simper (11)
Mount St Mary's College, Spinkhill

TRUTH

THE FISHER-BATSMAN

Truth

The old sailor walks in to take his guard
With memories fresh of his boat 'The Mallard'
He looks up to see the bowler at the end of his run
How he wishes he was on the ocean bobbing in the sun
An hour in the nets normally provides a wholesome catch
But this is the season's most important match
He knows the speed demon will bowl a tight line
Captain stood at the other end nods and says, 'You'll be fine.'
The new red cherry swings down swift and true
Fishing outside the off stump is what the batsman will do.

Matthew Fidler (11)
Mount St Mary's College, Spinkhill

THE RAILWAY

Truth

All my life I have lived near
To the railway which to me is so dear
I stood to see their cars so vast
And on the bridge to see them go past
In my dreams I travel
Zooming fast on the grey gravel
Flying through the morning mist
I would sit down and have a crisp
I get off two hours later
And on the other side see a freighter
Off the platform is the tube
That excited my mood
All fast and small
We squeeze in tight like a maul
On our way, to whatever is our place
The railway.

Christopher Penny (11)
Mount St Mary's College, Spinkhill

TRUTH

THE CALL OF AUTUMN

Truth

The trees are in tears for autumn has come
Their green, delightful coats are turning brown and yellow
The sun blends in
And it starts to look like the whole world is on fire
As fish take a cool swim in the river
The water rattles with laughing and dancing
As the bonfires rage on the Earth
The dark sky is full of shimmering sparkles
The streets are paved with child-shaped ghosts and ghouls
Searching for Halloween delights.

Abraham Murra (12)
Mount St Mary's College, Spinkhill

TRUTH FOOTBALL

Dare

T rusting in everything
R espectful for all equipment
U nique at sport
T ry hard at everything
H elpful people

F antastic with friends
O verjoyed about the friends I have
O verpowering with my left foot
T ruthful in anything
B eautiful just like my family
A wesome at sport
L ove sport
L ay down and have a good sleep.

Henry Renshaw (11)
Mount St Mary's College, Spinkhill

DARE

ANIMALS OF EXTINCTION

Dare

I have no home
I live alone
I have no teeth
They were taken from me
Probably sold
Sent overseas

The climate change is real
And our habitat is a big deal
It's been taken away
We had no say
It's never to be seen again

Illness is a big problem too
Wiping out species like me and you
We need to act fast
Make our world last
And see the changes through.

Phoebe Robinson (11)
Mount St Mary's College, Spinkhill

IN A FIELD I WENT TO LONG AGO

Truth

I went to a field long ago when everything was taller
And I had little toes
I laughed, I cried with friends nearby
Close to a river with a bank on the side
We ate, we drank with our best friend Frank
We paced, we danced into a beautiful trance
Oh what a life years ago before President Trump was, well, you know
Today I visited the field again
How I would love to relive in that moment again of my youth.

Theo Moore (11)
Mount St Mary's College, Spinkhill

TRUTH

THE JUMP OFF

Dare

I'm in the jump-off
My nerves start to tingle
Butterflies in my stomach
I walk the course and decide the best route
I get on my favourite, Percy, can we do it?
We're up first
The instructor says the numbers of the jumps
The bell rings and we're off
I'm over the first
I can feel the tension of the horse
We finish
But is it enough?

Joseph Buzzeo (12)
Mount St Mary's College, Spinkhill

UNTITLED

Truth

Summer is gone, winter is here
I'm not sure I like this time of year
No more sun or swimming pool
Just a thick coat and back to school

But Christmas is coming with family around
Ice-cold air and snow on the ground
Golden turkey on my Christmas plate
The summer has gone but life is still great.

Emily Louise Hardy (11)
Mount St Mary's College, Spinkhill

TRUTH

DIFFERENCES

Truth

Does it really matter what qualities you have?
Does it really matter what colour you are?
Does it really matter if you're tall or small?
It's up to you, but let's see what difference this poem can do

If you're tall you can see out far and wide
If you're small you can always easily hide
If you're mentally hurt about it just give me a call
'Cause it doesn't really matter if you're tall or small

Does it really matter if you're black or white
It's only a colour no need to fight
Racism can always hurt you some way
But don't start worrying, it'll stop one day

Does it really matter what qualities you have?
Does it really matter what colour you are?
Does it really matter if you're tall or small?
Well, the answer is no, 'cause that's just who you are.

Megan Edmonds (12)
The Bewdley School, Bewdley

TIME TICKS BY

Dare

Silence. It filled the room
In the dead of night
Lit only by the full moon
I sat alone watching her sleep
But I'm not a monster
Just a machine making a beep

I'm magic. I slow down time
But I can't hear so everything's just a mime
But time ticks on - life ticks by
We all go on, believing we can fly

We all take for granted that we can hear, see and more
Have a chance to give options
And a chance to choose
But I sit still - watching time tick by
I want to know more, more and ask why

So why do you happily kill and hurt,
Treating people like they're just dirt?
Why do you disrespect, always wanting more?
Why can't you stop this, breaking the law?
Why do you own a gun? Is it just a bit of fun?
Face your fears as the cold kiss of death nears
I can't stop this - time's ticking by
Make your change or else you'll never fly

DARE

I can see the future, it doesn't end well
You'll be going through the door to Hell
So don't hit, don't hurt, don't bully or mock
You can stop this - but I can't
I'm a clock.

Isobel Horton (11)
The Bewdley School, Bewdley

WHAT DID I DO AND WHY?

Truth

Each day I quake in fear
Not wanting to ever go near
My enemy, my bully
He doesn't understand fully
I get scared to go to school
He makes me feel like such a fool
He pushes, he kicks, he makes me want to die
All I ever wonder is, what did I do and why?
His gang of friends make my life a mess
I wonder why, I can do all but guess
Is it because I am top in most things?
Is it because I can afford precious rings?
When I get home I cry in my bed
Forever wishing I was dead
My mum asks what's wrong, why am I sad?
Not being able to tell makes me so mad
So I lie
And all I ever wonder is what did I do and why?
He calls me names I can't repeat
He uses me so he can cheat
I know I am small, I know I am smart
When he bullies me it breaks my heart

TRUTH

So please tell me and don't lie
What did I do and why?

Lily Grace Stansfield (11)

The Bewdley School, Bewdley

DETERMINATION

Truth

Gymnastics is about learning
Don't ever say you can't succeed
Everyone makes mistakes
But that means you try harder to achieve!

Some days you may stumble
And others may laugh
Yet people don't realise that others are different
So don't listen and be daft!

You're a gymnast at heart
And that's all that matters
All your mistakes you learn from
Because you concentrate and don't chatter!

The competition is about to start
It's your turn and you're burning up red
You might not have come first
But be strong, try again and don't let a tear shed

You've got great determination
To be a gymnast like you
The skills you have matter to you
So don't worry about what others can do!

Lauren Jessica Baker (11)
The Bewdley School, Bewdley

TRUTH

BEAUTY

Truth

What do you call beauty?

Is it the make-up and the products
That we lather over our faces every day?
The eyeshadow, mascara and powder -
The mask of make-up we cover ourselves with
Just covers up your real beauty
And who we are fully.

But to me...

Beauty is the things we say
And the thoughts we think
That make people smile and laugh,
Beauty is the way you are kind and caring
And how you are inside
Not on the outside.

You should be happy with who you are
And what you are like,
Don't let anyone make you change,
You are all you've got to be,
Don't let anyone change that because...

You are unique,
You are special,
You are beautiful.

Lucia Tromans (11)
The Bewdley School, Bewdley

TRUTH

ANIMAL CRUELTY

Truth

Animal cruelty, just stop it
Ask yourself, why do it?

You just look like a fool
You may think you look cool

They looked up to you
They have feelings too

Why make them scared
When you could just give them a bed?

They can play with you
They can run with you

You can change it around
With them you can mess around

They just want a cuddle
Don't put them in a muddle

How does it make you feel
Just give them a meal

Give them a bath
Change their path

Sign up for training
They're just waiting

TRUTH

They feel like they're failing you
Like they're not good enough too.

Caitlyn McLachlan (11)

The Bewdley School, Bewdley

WAR

Dare

War! War! Why does it exist?
War! War! Commencing in the mist
People dead for no major reason
War is the deadliest season

They go away for almost a year
They all march with barely any fear
Soldiers are the bravest type
All of them know how to snipe

War! War! Why does it exist?
War! War! Commencing in the mist
People dead for no major reason
War is the deadliest season

They fire their guns with a steady hand
And wait for their allies to painfully land
Many relatives live with doubt
Wondering if they will make it out

War! War! Why does it exist?
War! War! Commencing in the mist
People dead for no major reason
War is the deadliest season.

Ryan Ward (11)
The Bewdley School, Bewdley

DARE

I KNOW WHO I AM, WHO ARE YOU?

Truth

I know who am, who are you?
It's hard being yourself, we understand
One girl's new to school
Getting bullied, feeling suicidal

Bunch of girls beat her to the ground
She's still feeling suicidal
Thinking, *what's next?*
Stood up, turned around, her worst nightmare with the nurse
Walked home, tears in her eyes

Got home, blocked out her mom
Straight to the bathroom where she stands
With the razor...
Listening to her mom bang the door

Started screaming, fell to the floor
Mom kicked the door down
Found her on the floor
911 on the phone, found what happened
RIP new girl at school.

Sophie Davies (11)
The Bewdley School, Bewdley

TRUTH

EQUESTRIAN

Truth

The wind whips our hair
Fences stand in our way and tear
They tear our skin to many shreds
They tear our dreams to multiple threads

Heavy hooves snap our toes
We travel through time watching our soulmates grow
Mouthfuls of dirt, grit and grass
Don't ever harass
An equestrian

We may be short or even tall
But just remember we're the bravest of all
We work as a team with a half ton animal
It's a horse of course, a very large mammal

We are equestrians
Strong and tough
We are equestrians
Equestrians, equestrians...

Eve Westbury (11)
The Bewdley School, Bewdley

TRUTH

BULLYING

Dare

The tears roll down his face,
The blood oozes from his lip,
The bruises start to appear,
What has he done wrong?

The nasty words swirl around his mind,
The flavour of blood is still strong,
The sores are nearly healed,
But it keeps happening!

The tears still come,
The blood still oozes,
The bruises still appear,
They don't see what harm they're doing to the heart!

Inside hurts the most,
All the comments and strain,
All he wants from this world,
Is to stop the hurt and pain!

Charlie Davenport (12)
The Bewdley School, Bewdley

WORRIES OF THE WAR

Truth

Germany Vs England
The battle begins
Thousands of deaths
But after that, who wins?

Standing with your weapon
Looking brave about what to do
But inside you're petrified
As the next shot might be for you

An evacuee is running
Wondering what is going on?
I was sure Mum was with me
But when I turned around, she was gone

Soldiers standing in trenches
Tears filling their eyes
But it's not winning that they want
As seeing their families is the prize.

Leah Nicole Gittins (12)
The Bewdley School, Bewdley

TRUTH

I WISH YOU WERE STILL MY FRIEND

Truth

I wish you were still my friend
You talk about me
But you deny it
It's painful to know you were once my friend
I joke, I try, you think it's serious
Don't you know?
It's painful to know you were once my friend
I cry at night
I try to hide it, but I can't
It's painful to know you were once my friend
I tell teachers, they try to help
But you deny everything
It's painful to know you were once my friend
And after all this time
I wish you were still my friend.

Lydia Inchley-Jones (11)
The Bewdley School, Bewdley

TRUTH

A TRUE FRIENDSHIP BETWEEN HUMAN AND DOG

Truth

All dogs need is love
Nothing big to ask for
A pat on the head
A walk in the park
And a bowl full of food
All of that to keep
Them happy and healthy

A trip to the vet even
If it's a check-up
A nice day out
And remember to
Bond with each other

After all
You need a strong
And big friendship
With your dog
Because it's worth it

Most of all
No one lives forever

TRUTH

And you will only have one chance
To do that.

Anja Beau Scully (12)
The Bewdley School, Bewdley

TRENCHES YOU SEE

Truth

Bang!
This is the day it happened
Bombs blown
Bombs flown
Side to side
In the trenches you see
Rats!
Scavengers
But is that all?

Horses blown
Horses flown
Side to side
They've fallen into their final bed
But it that all?

Humans blown
Humans flown
Side to side
Humans are tied
To the ground
On no-man's-land
That's all!

Humans blown
Horses flown
Bombs no more.

Alfie Guy (12)
The Bewdley School, Bewdley

WAR!

Truth

The losses and the costs are really unbelievable
What it takes and what it gives you back
Is the complete opposite of each other
Every man is sent out to this wretched place
Will they come back or will they find their fate?

Out of nowhere I hear a screech
I have a peer on the beach
All our men lay dead
Some with bullets through their head
Then out of the corner of my eye
I see the one I feel like I could die

Bang... goes a gun
I run!

Tilly Harrison (11)
The Bewdley School, Bewdley

SCOOTING

Truth

The deck spinning, I feel like I'm winning
My eyes are focused on the prize
I do a flip followed by a backflip
I'm focused but I feel like I'm hopeless
The pressure is harder than ever, I pull a double flair with
lots of air
I throw a triple bar and go so far
My last trick is a master flip
I drop but it felt like it was a flop
I do a triple flair but fall right out of the air and smash
I have a massive crash
Which ends my scooting career.

Thomas Robert Ian Vick (11)
The Bewdley School, Bewdley

FOOTSTEPS

Truth

I hear footsteps
Coming my way
I head towards the sounds
I should have run away

I walk along the corridor
I suddenly stop
I see a shadow

I worry, I start talking
I start walking

My heart beats fast
I could have died
At least I'm still alive

I stand still
As if I am a statue
I don't know what I am doing
I am just staring into space
I hear more footsteps coming...

Lily Rose (12)
The Bewdley School, Bewdley

TRUTH

DEFORESTATION

Dare

Tell me who you think you are
Mercilessly destroying sweet nature
When all was calm - all at peace
You hurled our hopes afar

All we dreamt of; our pure imagination
Tossed and torn, broken and worn
Provoked in a hell of deforestation

Yet you still seem to think
You stubborn people know
That wildlife is unimportant
And not dripping with sorrow and woe

Deforestation
A demon gripping the nation.

Orla Southall (11)
The Bewdley School, Bewdley

PONIES

Truth

I love ponies
They are my thing
I have my own
That's all I need

I ride my pony every day
I kind of have to
I never let Mum ride any day
The only problem is...
Cleaning up poo!

I get him in
Groom him and clean him
Lead him
Ride him and jump him
You can't forget I love him!

All I need is another one
Just to do pony club
I love dressage
He is my pony
He is my dream!

Nell Howorth (11)
The Bewdley School, Bewdley

TRUTH

A CHILDHOOD DREAM

Truth

I started when I was only five
The sensation made me come alive
I played tag until age nine
Like a firework I began to shine

There seemed no end to my ambition
Achieving in life is my main ambition
But people tried to fill me with doubt
The one thing I can live without

When I make a tackle I do not flinch
Playing the game is a clinch
Rugby is what I want to do
Semi-finals down, now I'm coming for you.

Matty Gates (12)
The Bewdley School, Bewdley

WHY BULLY?

Dare

She's sat in the corner
Her eyes all red and puffy
Hoping for a hand to reach out

Wiping the tears she stood
With a ripped blouse and a missing tie

Muddy handprints all over her uniform
Scared of what was going to happen next

She felt awful when people were judging her for her
So why bully?
Just because they're different
Or your friends think it's funny
Stop and think, what if it was you!

Emma Louise Voysey (11)
The Bewdley School, Bewdley

DARE

THE BULLIED SHELF

Truth

An old book on the shelf far from timid
Sticking right out from where the last person put it
Covered in dust, smothered in words
Lost its fame due to its age
Gone out of fashion and never coming back
It's been all around the world, left, right and centre
Wherever there's people it's been there
In libraries they get called names for being in black and white
It's no different
They're no different
We're no different.

Harriet Cooper (12)
The Bewdley School, Bewdley

TRUTH

PANCAKES VS WAFFLES

Truth

Pancakes fight, fight for their lives
Against the evil waffles that terrorise the world
Impossible to defeat, impossible to eat
The German waffles now terrorise the world
With their Belgian chocolate sauce and their ice cream cannons
Now they're ready to defeat the waffles
And claim back what's theirs
Though they think they win, it is a close call
If they ate as much as they could
They would still be no match for the German waffles.

Reuben Dack (11)
The Bewdley School, Bewdley

TRUTH

A NEVER-ENDING BULLIED LIFE

Truth

A life full of anger, depression all from your sibling
Is a life of bullying, it never stops
My life is spent hiding from my brother
Hiding from the anger
Hiding and crying for hope
Yet all I have is my imagination
It never ends, no hope, just me
I sometimes have no confidence
So I just panic and sometimes I'm calm
I never know life is like a roller coaster
It's never-ending, I can never have fun.

Kelsee Lewis (12)
The Bewdley School, Bewdley

BLOODSTAIN

Truth

Crack! There goes the neck
Blood sprayed on the table like paint
He was almost dead
It crept towards us, two eyes stared at me
Lumps of red flesh lay on the ground
Organs thrown away, waiting to be found
With a knife through its neck
And with its insides out
He lay there lifeless
Small droplets of blood fell like water from an icicle
My hands stained with blood.

Nathaniel Champs (12)

The Bewdley School, Bewdley

TRUTH

SUNDAY

Truth

You wake up
To a lie-in
Then get ready for the sports
Get breakfast
A sausage sandwich
Get in the car
Turn the engine on, go
You can't be late
Or else laps
You walk on the pitch
The crowds roar

It's over, the joy over
You have your shower
Get changed, go to the table
Dinner's served
Then
You remember
Homework...

Nico James Bond (12)
The Bewdley School, Bewdley

THE BULLY PERSPECTIVE

Truth

It's another day
There's a guy in my way
Gonna punch him in the face
Make fun of his race
And put him into last place

It's time for our PE class
Throw him onto the grass
He ain't my mate
I'll give him lots of hate
We'll never be friends
Because this is one of those things that never ends.

Harry James Peter McIntyre (13)
The Bewdley School, Bewdley

TRUTH

THE BEAUTIFUL GAME

Truth

There goes the whistle
Studs as sharp as a thistle
Long ball into the box
Hunt it down like a fox

Find the ball at my feet
Through his legs
What a mess!
Managers writing me down on the first team sheet

Finesse it, top bins
50,000 fans screaming my name
Screaming my name in fame
The beautiful game...

Charlie Rutter (12)
The Bewdley School, Bewdley

MY HOBBY

Truth

When I go skiing
I do lots of spins
I always end up crashing
But that's how I do things

Skiing is my hobby
Though it can be stressing
I just pull right through
And try it all again

Sometimes it is painful
Sometimes it is not
But I just get back up again
Then do another flop.

Tom Annis (11)
The Bewdley School, Bewdley

TRUTH

CATS AND DOGS

Truth

All dogs need are treats
But the only thing they cannot eat, sweets
Also she sleeps in her bed
After she has had a pat on the head

They scratch on the walls
No idea what they are doing
Lying on the floor, thinking what to do next

Cats and dogs fight
Until it becomes night.

Charlie Wilson (11)
The Bewdley School, Bewdley

HERE THEY COME

Truth

Here they come
Just for fun, they kick and shove
I turn around but get knocked down
Just because they want a frown
I hear that sound, of the bell
Then I wait, behind the shed
Just waiting to be found

I hear a voice
It's my teacher
She asks what's wrong
I have no choice.

Ella Simmance (12)
The Bewdley School, Bewdley

TRUTH

FOOTBALL TRIALS

Dare

Kick-off time
All of the players want to shine
We wanna get signed

The managers in suits
We're in boots
Gonna work hard
Wanna turn out like Gerrard

Gonna pull out all the tricks
Hopefully score six

It's kick-off time
It's kick-off time.

Alex Franklin (13)
The Bewdley School, Bewdley

UNSUNG HEROES

Dare

They fight every day
For our peace
Every day they wait
For the hell fire to cease

They risk their lives
So we live in bliss
Whilst they await
Death's cold, cold kiss

Yet they lie forgotten
One of the many woes
Of being Earth's
Unsung heroes.

Eddie Millichip (12)
The Bewdley School, Bewdley

DARE

FORGOTTEN

Truth

They are voiceless creatures;
Incoherent echoes of the maimed souls
They had once possessed
Preserving their faceless ghosts
As ripples in your vision
Whispers in your ears
Umbras of the mausoleum
Imitate their phantoms
Their welded mouths closed
Their eyes noiselessly crying out
Their bodies trapped in the concrete walls
The forgotten stay here
Cast away by the grief of their families
With their souls that are tainted
By the experiences of a lifetime
Their lives a listless means to an end
This is where our demise occurs
No matter how prosperous your life was
Don't you find that daunting?
The idea of it all
Chills me to the bone.

Holly Farr (15)
The Elizabethan Academy, Retford

BLOOD OF A ROSE

Truth

Between two thorns
A rose has been born
A rose that's about to be torn
One that's about to make others mourn
A story yet to be told
This rose is yet to unfold
As people's bodies will start to get cold
The petals of this rose will never grow old
Knowing that this rise will make people cry
As it is the reason people are about to die
Is there a reason for this? If so why?
It's time the rose pays the price
What's happening is not nice
A simple apology will not suffice
After all it's happened more than twice
In hope of peace no one will find
With what is going through their mind
Innocent people that were so kind
All this positivity yet the rose was blind
As this rose starts to decay
The past started to fade away
Now it's nothing but a big display
But there's still a lot to say
So strong the soldiers stand

TRUTH

So blood-soaked are the noble hands
This bloodstained petal drips on the ground
As all endure this cacophony of sound
Sweet dreams turn to sour
As this may be their final hour
As the dawn breaks on another blood-drained day
We feel the cold wind with its gentle sway
Now that the Earth's an image of hell
The rose's colour starts to dwell
Now that the petals fell
Victims' family members start to say farewell.

Lexie Younger (14)
The Elizabethan Academy, Retford

NO ONE

Truth

Hurt, broken, alone
Horrible messages filled my phone
No one seemed to care
No one was there

Pushed out and moved away
Forgotten in just one day
No one seemed to care
No one was there

New friends, new people, new world
And still I'm that broken girl
No one seems to care
No one was there

On the road to recovery, progressing
Everyone is slowly forgetting
Still no one seemed to care
Still no one was there

My problems hid away in the shade
New friends were slowly made
Maybe they cared?
Perhaps they were there...

Happy, smiling, free!
Yes, the old cheerful me was coming back to see

TRUTH

People did care
People were there
You just need to find the right people.

Lauren Cross-Swain (14)
The Elizabethan Academy, Retford

GROWING CONTEMPLATIONS

Dare

Who says what is?
And who says what goes?
What is there beneath
The petals of a rose?

Who says what is?
And who can make flowers bloom?
Will there ever be a way
To preserve the Earth's greatest in one single room?

Who says what is?
And who can feel nature's heartbeat?
Is there a method
To not admire the sun's heat?

Who says what is?
And who says what and why?
Is there a story
Behind those who wither and die?

Who says what is?
And who can see life through a blind eye?
Can we ever tell
When to say goodbye?

DARE

Who says what is?
And who says what is possible?
Will my ever-busy path
Really be crossable?

Who says what is?
Who knows the cause?
Should every poor soul
Receive an applause?

Who says what was?
Who says what is?
Will the world ever
Be in perfect bliss?

Who says what will be?
And who knows what and whom?
Will the world
Ever stop to bloom?

Bethany Randles (13)
The King's CE (A) School, Kidsgrove

TORN YET STRONG

Truth

Relegation.
Discrimination.
A lion waiting for the kill.
Rearing on its hind legs,
Eyeing its prey,
Nowhere to run;
Nowhere to hide.
Glaring at me everywhere I turn.

Why must it happen?
My life is wounded because of it,
It hurts and it hurts.
Blood pounds in my ears as
I am judged like a book cover.

Torn apart and discarded.
I feel like leftovers that no one wants;
Chucked away in the bin,
Left to rot and
Mould away from everyone.

But then I remember.
A memory.
That strikes me all of a sudden
Like a fierce bolt of lightning.
I am not discarded.

TRUTH

I am not moulding.
Because I have a right:
The right of life, and a life that is good.
And I must use that right
Or leave it...

Risa Hope Clarke (12)
The King's CE (A) School, Kidsgrove

EQUAL

Dare

People
Intertwined in a world divided
Born together, swallowing their acid
Through your veins it runs
Unnatural

Unnatural
The word equality no longer meaning equal
A definition
Told and taught, accepted
Different

Different
The bars that separate us
Not known to mix
A broken programme
Unfixable

Unfixable
Cracks in humanity
Unable to see through
Unknowing what is behind the glass
Useeable

Useeable
The ability is gone
To see past what is not skin deep

DARE

They don't see us as the same
Indifferent

Indifferent
The way we were born
Before we were separated
We all breathe the same
Equal.

Georgia Rose Harley (14)
The King's CE (A) School, Kidsgrove

THE ROSE BETWEEN THE THORNS

Truth

Feeling forgotten
Feeling lost
Like a ball I am being tossed
I am almost popular
Almost famous
For all the wrong reasons
Their missions are not aimless

Standing by
Standing near
Adding to my deadly fear
My heart is torn
Beating fast
I wish their hatred would not last

See me for who I am
And not what you want me to be
To make yourself be better
Be famous, be me

Adding to the bruises and scars
They are from Earth
I am from Mars.

Paris Victoria Hilditch (11)
The King's CE (A) School, Kidsgrove

TRUTH

FREE

Truth

Freedom
Is a smile
Given on crossing paths

Freedom
Is the blue in my eyes
That's what you said to me

Freedom
Is the words you said to me

Freedom
Is my scars
That define me
That bind me to you
Just like my mind

Freedom
Is a flower
In fields of weeds

Freedom is as hard as the rocks
You threw at me
But as soft as tears you drew from me

TRUTH

Freedom
Is a light that touches
The darkness you gave to me

Freedom
Is a cage you put me in
With the blade free.

Trinity Olivia Jones (15)
The Priory City Of Lincoln Academy, Lincoln

TRUTH

ALZHEIMER'S

Truth

Do you remember when you were two?
Probably not, but your parents do
Do you remember when you were five?
Probably not, but I'm told you kicked a beehive
Do you remember when you were ten?
Probably not, but you had a boyfriend called Ken
Do you remember when you were twenty?
Probably not, but you fell out with your friend Jennie
Do you remember when you were thirty?
Probably not, but your life was sturdy
Do you remember when you were fifty?
Probably not, but you were quite crafty
Do you remember when you were eighty?
Probably not, but you had a nurse called Katie

I know you're trying hard Grandma, to remember all these things
But when you wake up, don't forget me.

Aimee Dilks (16)
Walton Girls' High School And Sixth Form, Grantham

GOLDFISH

Truth

A goldfish may forget
But can remember a lot
The things it does remember the most
Can be like being trapped in a spider's web
Unable to move, and do anything about it
Slowly devoured till there's nothing left

The goldfish was once in a bowl
Surrounded by other fish
That decided to die one by one, because, why not
And be taken out of the bowl, to another home
Because being with the goldfish was probably too boring
And still breathing and had a deeper meaning

To the goldfish the bowl was once a home, but eventually
became like a cage
Stuck seeing its own reflection for all eternity
Seeing everything from the sidelines, but not having the
power to do anything
Stuck just watching, never able to leave the cage
Forever alone
Until, the fish cannot breathe
Suffocating until it drowns

TRUTH

And, eventually, lose its golden colour, its only appeal
Until, it's just a fish
Everyone once admired the golden colour of the fish
But the fish has no appeal to it anymore
No one cares about the ordinary fish anymore
Forgotten, lost and alone
Dying quietly, like so many people once told it to
The fish once thought to itself, *why?*
But could never come up with an answer to why
And so, the fish that was once a goldfish met its demise
To the very end of its life
Forever alone and forgotten
Never thought about again
Until the end
And never again.

Cara Newton (15)
Walton Girls' High School And Sixth Form, Grantham

TRUTH

ANXIETY FORGOT TO INFLATE MY LIFE JACKET

Truth

On my way out I tripped over Organisation on the floor;
Grief clung to my side like a lost child and
Loneliness shuffled onto my shoulder, Love tugged on my hair but
Anger ripped her off and tossed her to the side,
Guilt lay flat, and still on my heart,
Tiredness retired to my eyelids and Awkwardness stood on my hands, wrapped his claw around my throat and shackled my lips shut
Sadness burdened me with a 42-kilogram weight,
Trust has butter fingers and today he lost his grip
Happiness uses me as a roller coaster but sometimes she forgets to strap herself in.
Anxiety forgets to inflate my life jacket

Hurt is an arsonist; today he burnt a hole in my head,
Boredom played with my lungs like Newton's cradle,
Efficiency's computer caught a virus and
Caution gambled and hop-scotched across my ribs, apologising to each one on her way
Confusion is struggling to solve the equation of M and E

TRUTH

Envy stole two handfuls of oxygen, and Empathy cleans up
everyone else's mess
Ugliness demolished every mirror in sight and
Jealousy hoards each and every particle,
The Past is an unwanted recurrent salesman
and Worry swallowed me whole.

Millie Grace (15)
Walton Girls' High School And Sixth Form, Grantham

THE LITTLE THINGS

Truth

It's hard sometimes
To do the little things
Waking up in the morning
When a million little men are talking at once
Smiling becomes difficult too
Something you used to do without even trying
It's the little things that are the hardest to do
Putting on a confident face
It's like painting on your clown face
Even in your pace
It's like everyone's thoughts are chained to your feet
It's the little things that are the hardest to do.

Abbie Webster (15)
Walton Girls' High School And Sixth Form, Grantham

TRUTH

YoungWriters
Est. 1991

YOUNG WRITERS
INFORMATION

We hope you have enjoyed reading this book – and that you will continue to in the coming years.

If you're a young writer who enjoys reading and creative writing, or the parent of an enthusiastic poet or story writer, do visit our website **www.youngwriters.co.uk**. Here you will find free competitions, workshops and games, as well as recommended reads, a poetry glossary and our blog.

If you would like to order further copies of this book, or any of our other titles, then please give us a call or visit **www.youngwriters.co.uk**.

Young Writers
Remus House
Coltsfoot Drive
Peterborough
PE2 9BF
(01733) 890066
info@youngwriters.co.uk